HAUNTED
COLLEGES & UNIVERSITIES OF
MASSACHUSETTS

RENEE MALLETT

Haunted
America

Published by Haunted America
A Division of The History Press
Charleston, SC 29403
www.historypress.net

CONTENTS

CONTENTS

DISCLAIMER AND WARNING

This is a book of real-life ghost stories and other paranormal or otherwise unexplainable occurrences that have been reported to happen at colleges and universities all over the state of Massachusetts. Many of the stories are based on first-person accounts, and some of the cases are quite famous and have been reported both online and in other books or magazines as well. Most of the stories, like all great ghost stories, have an element of local legend or folklore to them, and they walk the thin line between fiction and fact.

This book would not exist without the generosity of the people who decided to share their experiences, and as the old saying goes, many of the names have been changed to protect the identities of the people involved.

Please keep in mind that all of the places written about in this book are real schools that offer you, the reader, the opportunity to go and visit yourself. That being said, all of these places are institutes of higher learning. Before visiting any haunted site, remember that the people living, learning and working in these places deserve respect and privacy first and foremost. Never trespass; always get permission before you decide to go ghost hunting or to visit a haunted site. All ghost hunters are legally responsible for their own actions.

Many schools embrace their haunted histories, particularly around Halloween, and offer various lecture or walking tours where students and the public are invited to come learn about the college's ghosts and haunts. Even schools that do not hold these kinds of events themselves are often included in town walking tours. Boston and Cambridge in particular offer many of these ghostly themed events in the month of October. These kinds of events are a great way to learn about ghosts in your area in a very safe and legal way.

INTRODUCTION

I keep a workspace at Western Avenue Studios in Lowell, Massachusetts. Western Avenue Studios is one of many old mill buildings in the city that has been converted into new use, in this case into work spaces for artists ranging from quilters and painters to photographers and glass blowers. Along with the nearly two hundred visual artists who work in the building are the Loading Dock Art Gallery; The Space, which is both a café and a recording studio; and a small handful of writers like myself.

My studio is a calm sanctuary within this vibrant and colorful community of creative people. During the breaks between songs, I can hear laughter coming from Cultural Shock, the screen printers next door, or the soothing and rhythmic sound of fabric artist Tarja Cockell's loom on the other side. Throughout the building, there is always the sweet jingle-jangle of a dog leash as someone takes his or her pet out for a bathroom break. Sometimes in the middle of writing, I look up at my sea glass–painted walls and try to imagine what the factory workers who once put in long grueling hours in the old building would think of what we do here now.

There are many who say that the factory workers of yesteryear make themselves known to the current-day artists of Western Avenue Studios. And everyone in the building, it seems, even those who don't believe in ghosts, has had his or her own odd experience while working in the studios late at night or walking down the stairs to leave for the day. Being one of the rare writers in the building, and especially being one who is known for liking spooky stories, a lot of these tales filter their way down to me.

Artists come by the studio often while I'm at work to tell me their inexplicable experiences.

"I felt like someone had walked right into the room with me but..."

"And then I turned around and the paintbrush I had just put down was gone..."

"It must have been eighty degrees out that day, but all of a sudden a chill just washed over me..."

And I nod and say, "Yes, I have heard of that before. Yes, that is a classic sign of haunting. Yes."

Many readers who come to visit my studio during our monthly First Saturday Open Studio events like to joke that I must have picked Western Avenue Studios as my workspace just because "everyone knows how haunted these old mill buildings are."

And yes, there are a lot of ghost stories attached to these old factories. Workers put in long hours in the factories, arduous hours where accidents were the norm, and the bricks the mills were made of seem to be unusually receptive to holding the kinds of emotional energy that create long-term hauntings. But if spending years writing about the paranormal has taught me anything at all, it's that sometimes the most haunted places are the ones you'd least suspect of being haunted at all. In the course of my writing career, I've come across scarier ghosts in a newly built hair salon

than in an old Victorian cemetery and a brand-new apartment building that seemed to be more haunted than the old 1700s mansions that dot my little corner of New England. So while it might be easy to imagine a grizzled old millworker who died in some terrible factory-related accident groaning up and down the now bright hallways of Western Ave Studios, you are much more likely to run across spooky spirits in the more or less modern hallways of the ever-expanding University of Massachusetts in Lowell.

The two universal truths I have come to regarding true ghost stories are:

1) Police officers know the best ones.

2) You'll never find a library or theater without a good ghost or two hanging around.

If there's a third truth, and there probably is, it's that colleges and universities have the most ghost stories of all because, hey, they usually have at least a library on campus, and a lot of times they have theaters, too. Plus, they keep their own campus security officers around who can tell me the tales after the fact.

That doesn't mean that writing a book about campus spirits is an easy task. The thing about ghost stories on college campuses is that they tend to be a lot more legend than anything else. This goes doubly in Massachusetts, where the colleges are, usually, very old institutions.

Imagine the possibly very real sightings of ghosts on a college campus as a very long and disjointed game of telephone. One person thinks he sees a ghost; he tells his roommate, his best friend and also the cute freshman girl in his math class that he's been trying to find a way to break the ice with but hasn't yet been able start up a conversation. Two years later, the eyewitness has graduated, but the girl who looked so cute acing all the math exams is still in school. She mentions to an incoming student the story about the guy who once tried to hit on her with what had to be the stupidest pickup line ever—something about a ghost he was supposed to have seen in his dorm room one night. The incoming student thinks it's a pretty funny story, so she tells it to several of the people in her building. But to make it even scarier, she sets it in their own building, not the men's dorm on the other side of campus.

Now, times this by several decades. The story grows with each retelling; it gets moved around campus, the names get changed and the date becomes extremely vague. By the time a diligent author comes along to write about the building that "everyone on campus knows is haunted," it's impossible to sort out where or how the story started to begin with.

College legends are rife with tales of ghosts of suicides of former students, lovers who were killed, staff who hanged themselves somewhere on campus. All in all, there are almost never any mentions in newspaper articles or campus histories to back these stories up. If even half the urban legends about student suicides or campus killing sprees were true, no one would ever go away to college. The mortality rate for college students would be astronomical. Then, add in that the events in the ghost stories on campus happened, vaguely, "years ago," "a long time ago" or "back in the old days."

Does that mean the ghost themselves aren't real (assuming of course that you believe in ghosts to begin with)? Of course not. To repeat the old adage: where there's smoke, there's usually fire. These types of urban legends about a

Photo courtesy of Jessica Novak.

suicide that happened a long time ago are often invented just to make sense of the unexplainable. The building that everyone knows is haunted could very well be teeming with all kinds of energies and spirits; the unverifiable tales of suicide and madness were created out of the need to explain why students, people who didn't know one another, people reaching across decades, were all experiencing the same strange phenomena in the same place for no good reason.

This book collects the popular legends that have sprung up around college campuses all over the state of Massachusetts. Whenever possible, whenever something concrete exists, a mention is made of as much of the history and verifiable facts as can be found. And if none came to light in the course of research and writing? Well, that's okay, too. The stories reveal, in many cases, the odd histories that many colleges have, the strange disasters that sometimes struck them over the years and the darkest fears of students who are, in most cases, leaving home for the first time and striking out to create lives of their own.

And really, that's the best part about ghost stories. They might be true. Or they might just be a good story. Part of the reason why students across generations have been telling the same tales, handing them down from upperclassman to incoming freshmen, is because the stories themselves are worth repeating whether the teller believes in the ghosts or not.

HOW TO TELL IF YOUR SCHOOL IS HAUNTED

Never fear! Just because your school isn't included in the upcoming chapters doesn't mean that it's not haunted. While some colleges have ghost stories that are big news and get passed around from generation to generation, other schools have much quieter ghosts.

Whether you've experienced something unusual yourself and you're trying to track down the story behind it or you're a wannabe ghost hunter who wants to find out about the spooks and specters with which you're sharing your college years, there are a lot of ways to find out if your campus is haunted.

Do Your Research

With the recent rise in popularity ghosts and ghost hunting have seen in recent years, it is easier than ever to find local haunted places. The Internet is a good place to start. Google your school name along with the word "ghost" or "haunted," and that should start you off in the right direction. If your college library doesn't contain many volumes of true-life ghost stories, check out the local public library. Many colleges and towns have deals worked out that allow college students access to the books in the town library.

Photo courtesy of Jessica Novak.

Ask Around

In many schools, there seems to be a faculty or staff member who becomes the default school historian. Even if they don't have a particular interest in ghost stories, they usually know the history of the buildings and all of the local campus legends. The trick is finding out which faculty member you need to talk to. This is where your campus librarian will come in handy. Let him or her know you have an interest in the history of the school, and he or she can usually let you know which faculty member to talk to. The library may also contain an archive or special section on college history.

Historical Societies

Ghost stories are funny things. Like many hotels and restaurants, some schools embrace their legends and even promote them. Other schools do everything they can to keep them under wraps, whether out of a disbelief in the afterlife or because they don't want to distract or panic their students. But nearly every town, no matter how small, has a historical society of some kind. These organizations are often full of a wealth of information about haunted buildings in the town, up to and including the local college or university.

Call in the Ghost Hunters

Ghost-hunting groups abound these days. And many of them would love to be invited to your college so they can investigate possible hauntings. If your school is at all open about its ghost stories, you might be able to convince it to invite a local reputable ghost-hunting group onto campus. Many schools hold these kinds of events in the weeks leading up to Halloween. Generally, ghost-hunting groups will be willing to do a lot of the legwork for you, if you're willing to share the information you've come up with on your own. Their research can probably help fill in the holes.

Hold Your Own Investigation

Forget about fancy equipment. With a small amount of research, you can host an investigation of your own, even if all you're armed with is your own cellphone. If you've got a smart phone, and these days most college students do, you have a camera and an audio recorder and can download a free EMF reader app. And with those three things, you are armed and ready to find some ghosts of your own.

Be Skeptical

To paraphrase Occam's razor, the simplest answer is usually the correct one. When it comes to tracking real paranormal phenomena, the thing to keep in mind is that if there is a non-ghostly answer, that's probably what you're experiencing. If you are trying to track down real ghosts on campus, or want some kind of proof of the afterlife and want to have any hope of convincing others that what you had was a true uncanny experience, you have to think like a skeptic. Is the groaning you hear every night at nine coming through the walls the sound of a tortured soul or the sound of water running through the pipes as your neighbor takes a shower? Is that cold spot you feel in the library the spectral remains of a dedicated librarian or just a drafty window? Only after you have eliminated every rational explanation as a possibility can you even start to consider a paranormal one.

MIND THE CLOCK

It's a funny thing about hauntings. Everyone has this idea that ghosts, like vampires, werewolves and lazy undergrads, only come out at night. Not true! There are plenty of wonderfully haunted places that would positively bore you at midnight but would send chills up your spine at two o'clock on a sunny Tuesday afternoon. There have even been cases where the weather has affected how and when hauntings occur. Hauntings are very particular things. Each is unique and happens in its own way at its own time. If "everybody knows" a building on campus is haunted but you can't uncover any kind of phenomena yourself, try going at different times, in different seasons and on different days. Persistence might pay off.

KEEP A JOURNAL

This doesn't have to be a detailed diary about everything you did and how you did it. But keeping track of what you experience can be very helpful. Noting the day, time, the weather, what happened and who was there and what they experienced can help you determine a lot of things. It might help you figure out that what you're experiencing has a very rational cause or that your ghost is tied to a particular set of circumstances.

WORDS OF WARNING

It probably goes without saying, but there are some caveats to ghost hunting on campus. Always put safety first, and do not go poking around locked or abandoned buildings. Just because you are a student at a school doesn't mean you won't get slapped with a trespassing charge and possibly get yourself thrown out of school. Bring a friend. Never mix ghost hunting and alcohol or drug use. Consider all college and university rules and prohibitions before going ghost hunting. If in doubt at all, get permission from the proper officials first.

WHAT TO DO IF YOUR SCHOOL IS HAUNTED

Here's a dirty little secret about living with ghosts: they're actually pretty boring. Once you get past the initial fright factor, most people find there's nothing creepy at all about sharing space with the dearly departed. Many people say they get used to their ghostly roommates or find out that they can actually be pretty helpful.

As you'll see in the coming chapters, though, this isn't always the case. Some ghosts are noisy, troublesome, frightening or possibly even dangerous. And even the ones that aren't any of those things sometimes run right up against people who are just never going to accept how mundane they really are. If you are one of those people or if you run into one of these more extreme cases of haunting, there are some things you can do to make life more bearable for yourself through your college years.

Have you ever tried talking to a ghost? Believe it or not, some people who have come face to face with the frightening specters have tried doing just that—and have found that it is the simplest and easiest way to ease the pains of a haunting. In many cases, the things you're experiencing, even the most fearful of things, comes from the ghost's anger or frustration at not being acknowledged. Just by talking to the ghost, you're putting it at ease.

If that just doesn't work, or if you still can't get over the idea that the spirit of a dead person is sharing your room, talk to someone at school about moving. You don't even have to bring up the ghost if you're embarrassed. Colleges and universities know that there's a lot of competition out there for students. This goes doubly in Massachusetts, where there are so many schools you could transfer to that wouldn't even require a major move in location on your part. Schools want to keep the students they have happy. Most schools seem to have procedures in place to help students find the best possible rooming situation for their years on campus. You may have to wait for the semester to end, but chances are good you will be able to move into a more suitable, and non-haunted, dorm room if you ask.

As a last resort, you can always call in the professionals. Yes, that's right, there are plenty of ghost-hunting groups or other organizations that offer "cleansing" services. Sometimes this can be as simple as a medium coming in and talking to the ghost for you. Others claim to eliminate spirits completely. One group in New Hampshire that does this kind of work counts real estate agents as their biggest customers. Of course, this gets a little trickier when you're talking about your room on campus and not your own house. And the cost would no doubt come directly out of your own pocket. But considering how much college costs these days, and how important doing well in college is to your future, you can't put a price on peace of mind.

ANNA MARIA COLLEGE

PAXTON

Anna Maria College is a coeducational liberal arts college located in Paxton, Massachusetts. Its 1,600 students are spread across thirty-five undergraduate majors, twenty-one graduate majors and a handful of continuing education programs. Like many colleges offering majors in the performing arts categories, Anna Maria College has its own theater right on campus. And like nearly all theaters, Anna Maria's Zecco Preforming Arts Center is said to have its own ghost in residence.

It's hard to say why tradition holds that all theaters tend to be haunted. The theater community itself is full of superstitions, and the old adage that all good theaters are haunted may be just another example along the lines of saying "break a leg" instead of "good luck." It may be because of the emotional life of a theater, filled with big personalities and drama imprinting itself on the materials used to create the building. Of course, it could also simply be a trick of acoustics. An empty theater has the ability to magnify even the smallest noise into something much scarier sounding than it really is.

Theaters tend to embrace their haunted status. Many theaters keep one light burning in the center stage area when everyone goes home for the night. This ghost light, as it is known, either keeps the ghosts away or keeps them happy, depending on whom you ask. The ghost light does serve one very practical purpose, though: it keeps anyone wandering around after dark from stumbling off the edge of the stage and into the orchestra pit. Theater folk tend to like their ghosts. In many theaters, it's considered good luck for a production if a ghost stops by to watch a rehearsal. London's famous Palace

Theater keeps two seats permanently open for any ghostly audience members that might want to stop by and catch a show. The Zecco Performing Arts Center at Anna Maria College doesn't go quite so far in trying to appease its resident spirit, but the young woman, who is affectionately known as Theresa by the students, is a popular legend told around campus.

"They found a skeleton under the stage," Kelly said, eyes growing big. "Like, they were doing renovations and they found it. That's how we knew the ghost stories everyone was always saying were true."

It's something you'll hear again and again from former and current Anna Maria College alumni. Everyone, it seems, knows about the school once finding a woman's skeleton in the theater hidden beneath the stage. You'll also hear that the skeleton was found in the 1980s, the 1950s, that it was two hundred years old; that it was dressed in a flapper costume, dressed in Victorian dress; that it featured marks consistent with a stabbing; that the skull was bashed in violently; that the skull was missing; and, more rarely, that the skeleton was holding the tiny remains of a newborn baby.

Likewise, Theresa (or is it Maria? The name also depends on to whom you talk) is a former actress, a scorned lover, a betrayed wife, searching for her child, forced to live out eternity for harming her child or stuck on this plane forever until she finds her missing skull.

While the story behind this spirit is constantly evolving, as ghost stories tend to do, the activity that has sparked all the interest continues unabated while the debates rage on. The ghost has a fascination with modern technology, and many a student has rued the day that Theresa turned her attention to the theater's lights or the lead actor's cellphone.

Students aren't the only ones who get to enjoy Theresa's company. Audience members have been surprised to feel a small icy hand grip their shoulders during performances or to feel the presence of someone walking past them to an empty seat even while they can plainly see that no one is there.

If there's a ghost haunting the Zecco Preforming Arts Center at Anna Maria College, she's not alone. The music building at the school has a resident ghost of its own that students know as Betty. Betty has no known origin; there are no discovered skeletons, real or imagined, in this case. But what is known about her is that she loves playing the piano. The grand piano located in this building will strike up music without a player—or at least, no player that anyone can see. It's said that even when the piano's fallboard is closed, and even when it has been locked shut with a clamp, it doesn't stop the ghost from periodically tapping away at the keys.

BABSON COLLEGE

WELLESLEY

At first, the murmur of voices didn't do much to disturb David's slumber. He'd been studying all night, and even though Bryant Hall was one of the smaller dormitories on campus, he had gotten used to the noises associated with living with fifty other people. But eventually, the sounds escalated into what was, clearly, a card game getting out of hand. He could hear people arguing over the cards, clanking glasses and hooting when someone played a particularly good hand.

He was finally roused all the way from sleep by the smell of smoke. Cigar smoke to be exact. Whatever else was going on in the room next door, smoking was definitely taking things too far. David hauled himself from bed, pulled on yesterday's jeans and stomped out his door, slamming it loudly—a warning to the nearby gamblers.

In the hallway, David could hear nothing. It was late, late enough that the rest of the students at Babson College's Bryant Hall all seemed to be asleep, undisturbed by the late-night poker game that had roused him from his bed. He paused. How could he no longer hear the gathering

that had been loud enough to wake him moments before? Where was the smell of smoke?

Experimentally, he walked along the hallway, pausing to listen carefully at each door as he passed. David heard a few quiet noises from fans or music playing softly inside but certainly no large groups of students up all night partying. He was confused but happy not to have to be the one to break up anyone else's fun. Shrugging off the strange occurrence, he trudged back to his room, ready to get some sleep.

As soon as David opened his own door, he was greeted by billowing mists of thick gray smoke and the strong smell of cigars. Looking in, he didn't see his small dorm-sized bed or the desk where his laptop should have been sitting open, a half-written term paper waiting to be finished hiding behind his screensaver. Through the cigar smoke–induced haze, he could see several indistinct figures sitting around a table and laughing silently. He could see the card game, vaguely, but it was like watching a movie with the sound muted. David could see the players' mouths moving, heads thrown back in laughter, but it was all silent now. There were cards spread out around them; the table was scarred and dotted with cups and ashtrays. None of the players seemed to notice he was standing there.

Bryant Hall is one of the smallest residencies on campus, but one student found it had a room full of ghosts.

In shock, David took a step back and looked frantically around the doorway. He hadn't miscalculated—it *was* his room. But what had happened to his stuff? And who were these people?

The door slammed shut, startling him even more. David squared his shoulders and prepared himself to tell off what had to be a group of students playing some sort of unimaginable prank.

David flung the door open. He saw his bed, the sheets rumpled from sleep, his desk with its stacks of paper that needed organizing, the corner of the room filled with a few piles of clothes that he hadn't bothered to put away. The card players, the noise and even the lingering smell of their cigars were nowhere to be found.

He would never see the card players again, but a few times over his four years in Babson's MBA program, he would suddenly smell cigar smoke faintly and would be gripped by fear that he was about to come face to face with the unexplainable once again.

BERKLEE COLLEGE OF MUSIC

BOSTON

Berklee College of Music is the world's largest independent school of contemporary music. One of the school's claims to fame is that ninety-nine former Berklee students have gone on to win 229 Grammy Awards among them. Brad Whitford of Aerosmith, Natalie Maines of the Dixie Chicks, Rashawn Ross of Dave Matthews Band and PSY of "Gangnam Style" fame are all Berklee College of Music alumni.

As with many of Boston's finest colleges, Berklee College of Music started off small and grew as the years passed by. Originally, the school was housed in just one small building on Newbury Street. As time went on, the school moved into a larger building on Boylston Street, the site of a former hotel. Then, beginning in the 1970s, the school went through a period of rapid growth that saw the purchase of several surrounding buildings in the neighborhood. One of these was the Fenway Theater, which was renovated and reopened as the Berklee Performance Center in 1976; another early addition to the Berklee College of Music campus was the Sherry Biltmore Hotel.

The Sherry Biltmore Hotel was once a Boston landmark complete with stores, ballrooms, lounges and a beautiful center courtyard. But the Sherry Biltmore Hotel's once grand history would be marred with a disaster. In the predawn hours of March 29, 1963, a fire ripped through the nearly full-to-capacity hotel. It began in room 655, which was unoccupied at the time, and it is unclear how long the fire was allowed to spread unchecked before guests began complaining of smoke. When the first calls started coming in to the front desk, a bellboy was sent to investigate while hotel management went to the top floors to calm the guests.

Like many colleges in Massachusetts, Berklee College of Music bought the buildings around it as it expanded, creating many opportunities for current students to have run-ins with historic residents.

While fire and smoke poured out of room 655, cast members from *The Sound of Music*, which was being performed at a nearby theater, partied in suites 603 to 611. When a young actress opened the door to one of these suites to try and air the cigarette smoke from the room, she was surprised to find the hallway even more clogged with smog than the party was. By this time, the entire hallway was choked with flames. In a panic, *The Sound of Music* actors and stagehands began breaking windows in the suites, and about forty of them climbed out onto a very narrow window ledge to await the fire department. One panicked partygoer had the foresight to pull the fire alarm as he went out the window, but it was to no avail. While the alarm alerted the rest of the hotel guests about the fire, driving them into a panic but probably saving many lives that would have otherwise been lost, the alarm wasn't connected to the Boston Fire Department at all.

A Boston police officer who just happened to be passing by on his rounds did a double take when he saw the large numbers of people climbing from the hotel windows. He noticed the flames a second later. Realizing that the Sherry Biltmore Hotel was under duress, he quickly radioed for all available ambulances and fire personnel. By the time the fire department arrived, it found a nightmare scene waiting. Black smoke billowed gaily from broken windows while an untold number of hotel guests, all in various states of undress, took refuge on window ledges and small sections of nearby roofs. The department carried nearly eighty hotel guests down the ladders that night. Ultimately, four people would die in the fire, or from the effects of smoke, and an additional twenty-five were injured.

Considering the horrific fire that took place in the building, it should come as no surprise that some guests are still caught up in the flames, reliving that terrible night, long after they have passed. At least one dorm in the Massachusetts Avenue building has a ghost that is obsessed with water. Students who have lived in this dorm say that the sink turns itself on and runs nonstop while water pours from beneath the doors and soaks the hallway. No matter how often they turn the faucet off, they inevitably come back to their rooms to find it running again. In this room, even the toilet flushes on its own, a minor occurrence but one guaranteed to break your concentration while studying or to wake you up when you're trying to sleep. A few more sensitive students who have slept in this room also claim to have seen the ghost with their own eyes. The figure they all recount is eerily alike, although none of the witnesses knew one another. The ghost is described as a young woman wearing a filmy nightgown and with an unusual style of sleeping cap still perched on her head.

Many in the former Sherry Biltmore Hotel building claim to be plagued by a weird bluish colored smoke that irritates their eyes even while others around them say they see nothing. Students throughout the building hear frantic knocking on their dorm room doors by an unseen person, presumably a concerned spirit trying to alert them to a fire that no longer exists. More active spirits have been seen beckoning for help from outside the windows. Sounds of breaking glass without a definite cause are not uncommon.

BOSTON COLLEGE

CHESTNUT HILL

"Every now and then I'll be lying in bed and see this little dog sitting under my desk looking at me," Feven Teklu, a former Boston College student, told a staff writer for the campus paper in 2002. "It's there and then it disappears. It's kind of eerie and definitely a mystery."

Teklu isn't the only student to discover that things are a little off in Boston College's O'Connell House. The beautiful building, laughingly called the "haunted mansion" around campus, was built in 1895 by the Storey family. It was modeled after Gywdr Hall in Wales. For much of the building's history, it was the estate of the Liggett family, and many of the ghost stories that survive to today are thought to be linked to this time. Eventually, the family donated the home to the archbishop of Boston. Three years later, he turned around and donated it himself, this time to his alma mater, Boston College.

Boston College originally used O'Connell House, named after the man who donated it, as classroom space. Eventually, it became a residence hall. Today, it is used as a student cultural center for the campus, housing social events and entertainment for the students who live on campus. In its current usage, there aren't as many reports of ghost stories. Nearly all the encounters with spooks, spirits and things that go bump in the night happened when the ghosts were living shoulder to shoulder with students on a daily basis.

The ghostly little dog is just one of several spirits that students have encountered over the years at O'Connell House. The most active is a female spirit that resides in the mansion's attic. Popular legend says the girl was a member of the Liggett family who was kept locked in the attic for an extended period of time, either as punishment for a love affair, to hide the unwanted pregnancy of an unmarried daughter or to hide her mental illness and save the family's reputation. In death, this woman has a hatred for locked doors and windows. Students have found that locking anything, even desk drawers, seems to draw the attention of the spirit. When students returned from classes, they would find their previously closed doors thrown open and locked desks shoved around the room angrily.

Much of this ghost's anger was turned toward the windows in the very attic where she is said to have been imprisoned so long ago. Even today, people in the building can hear the sound of the attic windows being hastily opened and slammed shut, even though the attic is empty and kept locked for safety reasons. The sound of the opening and shutting windows is even more surprising considering that the attic windows in O'Connell House no longer open at all. Years ago, they were changed out to a fixed single-pane glass, yet the sound of the windows opening and shutting persists.

Another popular ghost story linked to O'Connell House's days as the Liggett family estate says that Mr. Liggett discovered his wife was having an affair and killed her lover. The love triangle continues to be played out today as the two men still fight for the hand of the woman they shared between them.

The building is also supposed to be as haunted on the outside as it is on the inside. The spirit of a five-year-old boy, rumored to have drowned in a pool that once stood outside the home's solarium, still wanders around outside O'Connell House. People have reported hearing the sound of a child laughing and playing when there was none to be seen. The boy is supposed to have a special fondness for children and to be protective of them. One student said that after his family visited him at school one fall, his younger brother, only five years old himself, talked about playing with a ghostly little boy outside O'Connell House that only he could see. The family passed it off as an imaginary friend until the little boy gave more details about his invisible friend's old-fashioned clothing, blue lips and dripping wet hair. Later, the student would hear the rumors about the ghost outside O'Connell House and put two and two together.

Several years ago, Lorraine Warren, noted medium and psychic investigator, was invited to O'Connell House by Boston College students. Boston College's student newspaper, *The Heights*, covered Warren's visit to the school. The clairvoyant described the energy in the thirty-two-thousand-square-foot building as, overall, very positive. She agreed there were several presences lingering in the building. In particular, Warren mentioned the ghosts of two grown women, a baby and a small dog.

O'Connell House has one unusual claim to fame that has nothing to do with spirits, human or canine. Several scenes of *13 Rue Madeleine*, a 1946 film starring James Cagney, were filmed in the building. The school was so proud of its ties to Hollywood that the movie played annually in the grand hall of the house for the students for many years. While the movie is no longer shown to students each year, movie rentals are provided for free to students in O'Connell House's latest incarnation as the school's student entertainment center.

A few other buildings at Boston College have gotten the ghost house moniker from time to time over the years, but none has the depth of stories that come out of O'Connell House. The building at 66 Commonwealth Avenue is said to have a few specters that date back to the building's original use as a retirement home, before it was bought by Boston College. In the true spirit of urban legends, the myth around campus has turned its rather prosaic start as an old folks home into a mental institution. While this may add some extra chills to the retelling of the tales, it obscures whatever truth might lie beneath that could offer some clues to the actual haunting.

Hovey House also has some whisperings of hauntings surrounding it. The twenty-year-old home is Boston College's Center for International Studies and the site of several faculty offices. As a whole, Boston College tends to deny its ghost stories. So if any of the faculty who keep offices in Hovey House have had the kinds of ghostly encounters a few students have hinted at, it is unlikely they would publicize them.

BOSTON UNIVERSITY

BOSTON

The ghost in Boston University's Kilachand Hall (a fairly recent moniker, as the building was formerly known as Shelton Hall for most of its history) is notable because he was just as famous in life as he is now in death.

None other than Eugene O'Neill is said to stalk the hallways of what is commonly known as the Writers' Corridor of the Kilachand Hall dorm. O'Neill was an Irish American playwright and the 1936 Nobel Laureate in

literature. Three of his plays, *Anna Christie* (1920), *Strange Interlude* (1928) and *Long Day's Journey into Night* (1941) would earn him Pulitzer Prizes. Despite his wild success as a writer, O'Neill was plagued by health problems throughout his life. In the last ten years of his life, the playwright was able to complete only a few works due to a heavy tremor in his hands that was misdiagnosed as Parkinson's disease. On November 27, 1953, Eugene O'Neill died in room 401 of the Sheraton Hotel in Boston, a building that would go on to become part of Boston University. Eugene O'Neill's last words as he died were reported to be: "I knew it. I knew it. Born in a hotel room and died in a hotel room."

What Eugene O'Neill didn't know was that the Sheraton Hotel where he spent the last unhappy years of his life would become a dormitory for Boston University just one year later, in 1954. He certainly never would have imagined that the school would rename the fourth floor of this building the Writers' Corridor in his honor. Popular legend says that O'Neill still walks the hallways, surprising unsuspecting students. Luckily, the benign presence of O'Neill seems to be more of a draw for Boston University than a spooky spirit to be avoided.

"Students have told me that they hoped to be inspired to write their creative best by virtue of being on the fourth floor. Others said they actually

Shelton Hall at Boston University is notable for having a spirit that was as famous when he was alive as he is in death.

wanted to connect with his spirit," David Zamojski, director of Residence Life and an assistant dean of students, told *BU Today* in a 2009 article about the well-known haunting. He then added that students in the residence hall "have been telling stories about O'Neill's spirit and ghost as long as I've been here. We have received reports of many a strange incident."

In fact, there were so many frequent incidences concerning O'Neill's ghost that for several years the Writers' Corridor featured a community bulletin board where students could write down and display the strange things that happened to them.

Many of the strange incidences can be passed off by skeptics as simply the effects of an older building that has seen a lot of use between its years as a hotel and its time as a college dorm. The elevator in Kilachand/ Shelton Hall stops continually on the fourth floor even when no one is there to press the button to call it. The lights are dimmer on this floor than any other, though when this is brought up, many cynics are quick to point out that for whatever reason, the ceilings in the Writers' Corridor are a little higher than in other parts of the building. Others report flickering lights, strange noises and even a toilet that flushed on its own long before the advent of motion detectors.

Some things seem to be more in line with college pranks than with ghostly activity. Students hear knocks on their dorm room doors in the middle of the night and find no one on the other side when they answer them. Other things are less easily explained. One longtime fourth-floor resident said that she and her roommate would feel, and hear, a large gust of frigid air blow under their door almost every night. They could never find the source of the cold air, and none of the students who had dorms around theirs ever reported feeling it. Many have complained of phones, including cellphones, that randomly dial, leaving long lines of fours across the screens.

Interestingly, the room that is said to be the room Eugene O'Neil died in has had the least amount of paranormal incidences reported. A student-led séance in the room also failed to stir up any ghosts. If Eugene O'Neill is still wandering around Kilachand Hall, he seems to be sticking to the corridor and not to the room where he spent the last several years of his life.

Kilachand Hall isn't the only haunted building you can find at Boston University. And O'Neill isn't the only famous ghost that is sometimes seen on campus. None other than Babe Ruth and the Boston Strangler are said to also haunt the school.

Myles Standish Hall has an eerily similar history to that of Kilachand Hall. It was built in 1925 as the Myles Standish Hotel. For many years, Myles Standish

Hotel was considered to be one of the finest in Boston—and the world. Its proximity to Fenway Park made it a favorite of all the famous baseball players of its day. However, popular as it was in its short-lived heyday, the Myles Standish Hotel was hit hard by the Great Depression. In 1933, it tried to remake itself as a fashionable Back Bay apartment building, but the concept wasn't as successful as it was hoped to be. In 1949, Boston University purchased the down-on-its-luck property and converted it into a dormitory.

Babe Ruth was one of the baseball luminaries who often stayed at the Myles Standish Hotel. He liked it there so much that he even had a favorite room, number 818, and asked that it be kept in reserve for his frequent visits. Nobody seems to have clued the Bambino in that these kinds of deals usually expire after death. The baseball player died the year before Boston University bought the building but has been seen often in the years since, wandering in and out of his favorite room. As far as ghosts go, Babe Ruth is supposed to be a fairly boring, but considerate, roommate. He doesn't have the same interest in dialing the number four on telephones that Eugene O'Neill's spirit has, and he doesn't knock on doors or walls at any hour.

Before being converted into a dorm, Myles Standish Hall was a hotel popular among the famous baseball players of its day.

Myles Standish Hall has a literary connection that nearly rivals that of Kilachand Hall's playwright ghost. An uncle of Arthur Miller, who is said to have been the inspiration behind Miller's Willy Loman character in *Death of a Salesman*, was once a resident of the building during the few short years when Myles Standish Hall was an apartment building. Miller's uncle committed suicide on the ninth floor. Students living on the ninth floor complain of a roving cold spot that likes to rearrange furniture while they're away at their classes. Students have come back to their rooms to find dressers and desks with their drawers hanging open and with the furniture in entirely new, and often unwanted, configurations.

As innocent as the ghosts at Boston University may seem at first glance, the school has ties to a much darker part of Boston's history. In fact, some of Boston University's ghosts are more infamous than famous. In the early 1960s, Bostonians were shocked by a series of murders that took place in and around the city. The city was under siege by a serial killer who entered women's homes, molested them and then strangled them with articles of clothing. The women targeted were not the usual types of victims that serial killers looked for. The initial series of victims were respectable women in their fifties and sixties. These were definitely not the easy targets most serial killers went after—prostitutes, runaways or those otherwise living on the fringes of society.

Eventually, Albert DeSalvo confessed to thirteen of the crimes that were credited to the serial killer the press had dubbed the "Boston Strangler." But even today, the case remains clouded in mystery. There are as many contradictions in the case as there are certainties. While DeSalvo was able to give the police a few details in his confession that were not public knowledge at the time, there was never any physical evidence linking him to a single one of the murders attributed to the Boston Strangler. Two of the women he said he killed were never previously considered to be Strangler victims at all. Even today, it is unclear just how many women were really killed by the Boston Strangler. A great deal of the evidence points to there having been several killers all acting under the same modus operandi at the time.

Those who knew DeSalvo thought he was incapable of the crimes. While the opinion of friends and family carry little weight when it comes to a man's innocence or guilt, DeSalvo would eventually have several of the world's leading crime experts publicizing their belief in his innocence. But DeSalvo wouldn't live to hear any of them cast doubt on his confession. In 1973, while serving a life sentence, he was stabbed to death by fellow inmates in Walpole State Prison. No one was ever arrested in conjunction with DeSalvo's murder.

Patricia Bisette was an unusual victim for the Boston Strangler. At twenty-three, she was significantly younger than any of the Strangler victims who had come before her. Bisette, a secretary at a local engineering firm, was found in bed, with the covers neatly pulled up to her chin, strangled by several stockings that had been elaborately knotted together. Bisette's body was discovered when her boss became concerned when she hadn't shown up for work in a few days. Her boss, with the help of a custodian at her building, broke into Bisette's apartment through a bedroom window.

Today, what was once Bisette's apartment building is housing for Boston University. Understandably, the school doesn't particularly advertise the building's unsavory history, but upperclassmen are always quick to point it out to the incoming freshmen each fall. While the university lore doesn't always get all the facts quite right, as there are swirling rumors at Boston University that the Boston Strangler lived in the building himself to others saying he killed all his victims in the apartment house over the course of one grisly night, everyone agrees the building is home to at least two haunts.

One of the building's ghosts is said to be that of a young woman who is generally assumed to be Patricia Bisette. She is often heard crying and then seen running frantically from an unseen pursuer. The other ghost is supposed to be that of her killer, though why he would spend eternity in an apartment where he killed this particular victim and not be seen at the site of any of his other crimes has never quite been explained. While no one who has seen the ghost has said yet if it looks like DeSalvo, many claim he is dressed as a maintenance man of some kind. It's a small detail but a chilling one to anyone who is familiar with the Boston Strangler case. Every one of the victims of the Boston Strangler is believed to have let their attacker into their apartments willingly, and it has long been believed that the killer disguised himself as a delivery man or maintenance worker in order to gain this access into his victims' homes.

BRIDGEWATER STATE UNIVERSITY

BRIDGEWATER

B ridgewater State University is the largest college in the Massachusetts state university system that doesn't have a "UMASS" at the start of its name. This liberal arts school needs the room—it's chock full of ghosts and specters of all kinds. The school sits inside of the famous Bridgewater Triangle, making it unsurprising that it has become known for its many strange occurrences.

The Bridgewater Triangle is a roughly two-hundred-square-mile area in southeastern Massachusetts that has become famous, though not quite as famous as the much more popular Bermuda Triangle, over the years for its plethora of paranormal activity. When it comes to the Bridgewater Triangle, we're not simply talking about a high incidence of ghosts or poltergeists. The Bridgewater Triangle has also seen many, many claims of UFO activity, weird lights and balls of fire, along with claims that the area is home to a range of cryptozoological creatures, including a big foot–like ape-man creature and a giant pterodactyl-like flying animal known as a thunderbird.

Of course, with so much attention being put on the uncanny happenings in the Bridgewater Triangle, there are also a whole host of other phenomena that sadly tend to go hand in hand with rampant tales of the supernatural. Animal mutilations occur at what seems to be a slightly higher than average rate in this area, though of course it could simply be that the cases that are reported make bigger headlines because of the Bridgewater Triangle connection.

In another chicken-and-egg type of scenario, the Freetown–Fall River State Forest, which is also located within the Bridgewater Triangle, has had some evidence of being a possible home to a satanic cult. A number of crimes have been linked to this group over the past few decades. Unlike most rumors of satanic groups or other cults, there are actually news and police reports to back these legends up. In the fall of 1978, the body of a missing fifteen-year-old girl was found tied to a tree in the forest. The police would catch a man they said had killed her, and that man, James Krater, would go through a series of trials and appeals that stretched into the 2000s. In the 1980s, the police would find another Freetown–Fall River State Forest connection in another well-publicized murder. This case resulted in several witnesses coming forward to tell authorities about the satanic cult activities that they had seen, or in some cases, taken part in, in that dark stretch of the woods. Over the next twenty years, police would find that three more local murders either happened in the forest itself or had ties to the cult that was operating out of it. Police records also show a series of assaults taking place in the forest, reports of a wild pack of feral dogs and, in a far more innocent but still quite memorable incident in 2006, the woods becoming home to an escaped emu.

Located just over fifteen miles away is Bridgewater State University. Luckily, the school boasts a much safer and slightly less colorful history than that of the Freetown–Fall River State Forest. But it certainly has more than its fair share of haunts. The Shea-Durgin Halls at Bridgewater State University are the site of several hauntings. The fifth floor of this residence hall is home to a can-stacking ghost that is commonly known as the "Poltergeist of Shea-Durgin." Most experts in the paranormal would disagree with the spirit's name. While the ghost that frequents the fifth floor has its hand in many poltergeist-like activities, such as the aforementioned can stacking and the rearranging of chairs, most experts have come to agree that a poltergeist is a very special kind of paranormal experience that probably has nothing to do with ghosts at all.

The term *poltergeist* translates to "noisy ghost." They are credited with such phenomena as unexplained knocking and rapping. Besides the noise, they can be temperamental, flinging around inanimate objects and, in some extreme cases, even pinching, biting or hitting the living humans they encounter. Poltergeist phenomena have been recorded in all cultures dating back about as far as we have written records. Historically, they were thought to be angry spirits or even minor demons.

Thinking about these kinds of poltergeist behaviors has changed rapidly in even just the past few years. Most experts are now of the opinion that poltergeists are not spirits at all, noisy or otherwise. The poltergeist activity almost always centers on one family member, in earlier times creating the impression that this person was cursed or had otherwise done something to deserve the ghost's anger. It is now thought that this type of phenomenon is something more like a spontaneous and uncontrolled telekinesis or psychokensis. In looking at the history of poltergeist activity, it quickly becomes clear that these types of hauntings occurred suddenly, more or less at the exact time that a child within the household being plagued by the noisy ghost hit puberty. Many believe this influx of changing hormones, and the resulting emotional distress, creates an environment where these kinds of wild talents act as a pressure gauge that relieve some of the mental tension. True poltergeist activity normally lasts only a fairly short period of time—a few weeks to just a few years in the most extreme cases—and seems to center on this pubescent person within the family before disappearing as suddenly as it had come.

The recent change in beliefs around poltergeists has done nothing to change the minds of the students who live and interact regularly with the ghost on the fifth floor of Shea-Durgin Hall. Whoever the spirit is, it is seen as an annoyance—though thankfully, only a very minor one. Unfortunately, the Shea-Durgin Halls boast at least two other ghosts that are much less easily tolerated.

A bathroom in the building is home to a ghost that can't seem to leave the showers alone. All in all, not a big deal. That is, unless you happen to be taking a shower that runs hot and cold all on its own and suddenly turns itself off or starts up without warning. Some students have reported seeing a black object moving around the bathroom just at the edges of their peripheral vision. There's nothing like being startled while you're standing around vulnerable and naked in the shower!

One of the second-floor rooms is the scene of a long-standing legend at Bridgewater State College. It is said that a young woman was choked to death by her boyfriend, who was convinced she was cheating on him. While there's not a lot of hard evidence to back the story up, you can find a plethora of students who will swear up and down that there's a dark energy in this particular room that just doesn't exist elsewhere in the building. Others who have slept in this room complain of being awakened by the sound of an unseen victim choking. Others would be happy to hear only a little gagging. Sometimes angry voices rise up from the room at nearly impossibly loud levels.

Students in Woodward Hall at Bridgewater State College could commiserate with those who have listened to the ghostly couple fighting.

They have been plagued for years by a ghost that runs up and down the hallways banging on doors and warning that a fire has broken out. When students leave their rooms, they find no one there and no scent of smoke. But the experience is so real that many have rushed all the way outside before realizing there's no emergency.

The ghost is thought to belong to a long-ago period in the school's history. Originally, Bridgewater State University was known as the Bridgewater Normal School back when it was founded in 1840. At the time, the school was dedicated solely to educating and training teachers. It wasn't until the 1960s that the school expanded its mission and also its program offerings.

In between when the school was founded and when it started its evolution into the university that exists today, a horrific fire ripped through the campus. The year was 1924, and at least four buildings, or roughly half the school as it existed at that time, were completely destroyed. One of the buildings that was reduced to ash and rubble was the Old Woodward Dormitory.

Few records exist today from the extensive rebuilding process the school underwent after the fire. Students and classes were moved temporarily into the surviving campus buildings, and in time the burnt buildings were replaced. It is unclear if the current Woodward Hall was built atop the remains of the Old Woodward Dormitory, but given the similarity in names and the few bits of archival records left, it certainly seems likely.

Popular legend has it that the unseen girl who sparks the hasty unplanned fire drills set the fire of 1924 herself. Historic records show us that no definite cause was ever found for the disastrous blaze. Ultimately, the school chalked the fire up to rodents gnawing at heating ducts near the boiler room, but it was never a conclusive ruling. It is always possible the girl had something to do with the conflagration and that the resulting fire covered whatever evidence she left behind. Now in death, she is trapped, playing out the accident night after night, long after the fire has been forgotten by the students on campus.

And as for the long-standing story that Woodward Hall's ghost died in the fire? Nothing more than urban legend that has grown from years of retelling. All records from the time agree that, miraculously, not a single student or staff member was injured or killed that night.

The co-ed housing located at the Great Hill Student Apartments has an extremely unpleasant manifestation. While the students in this building deal with the typical ghostly knocks and stomps that are common in haunted houses, a few select rooms also deal with much less tolerable phenomena. These students say they are randomly assaulted with the overwhelming stench of death and rot.

The smell doesn't seem to be linked to any particular activity on their part, or that of their neighbors, and it comes and goes suddenly. Many have complained to the school to no avail. It never happens on command, so maintenance workers don't experience the smell themselves, and no one has been able to find an earthly explanation for it. While one apartment is overcome with the smell, the one directly next door won't catch a single whiff of the terrible odor.

One of the most popular and benign spirits on the Bridgewater State University Campus is George. The stories don't say who George might have been in life, or even how anyone ever decided his name was George, but he tends to hang out in the Auditorium at Rondileau Campus Center. Like many ghosts, George has a habit of turning the lights on and off at inopportune times. He also likes to move theater props to inaccessible places and has been known to play the orchestra instruments from time to time.

The most important thing to know about George is that it seems like these happenings are because of his playful nature, not because he's out to scare or irritate anyone, although that does happen from time to time. Caitlin, a former Bridgewater State University student, said that she felt like George enjoyed the students who went along with his jokes. During her time in the school, she took part in many performances in the Auditorium and said that, just a few times, George came up against someone who took everything he did as an affront. And, says Caitlin, George then seemed to go out of his way to make these uptight people the targets of his pranks.

Complain about the ghost moving a prop and you're likely to have your copy of the script go mysteriously missing. Criticize George's musical ability and your spotlight will drop at a crucial moment. And unlike many ghosts, George isn't known for giving up the game when asked politely. Still, mostly everyone agrees that everything George does is all meant in good fun and that if a few people get peeved at his antics from time to time, at least he made a point of targeting the people who most deserved it.

CHARLESGATE HALL

BOSTON

Charlesgate Hall isn't a college or even part of a college, at least not anymore, but the sheer number of paranormal events that have been reported here and its historical use by two colleges in Boston has earned it a place in this book. The building was designed and built by John Pickering Putnam in 1890 as the Charlesgate Hotel. The Romanesque Revival building is currently the site of luxury condominiums in Boston's Back Bay neighborhood. In between its time as a hotel and a condominium, the building would serve as a dormitory for two separate colleges, as a boardinghouse and, it has long been rumored, as a den of ill repute, serving as both a bordello and a Mafia headquarters.

This ornate doorway may have once led into a Mafia headquarters and a bordello.

Left: It has been rumored that the Charlesgate was built specifically to be a paranormal hotspot.

Below: The carvings found liberally around the building are said by some to have been created with ghosts and spirits in mind.

Almost since its inception, the Charlesgate has been surrounded by ghost stories. In fact, the plentiful supernatural tales that take place in and around the building have been the subject of some rumors of their own. Christopher Balzano, a paranormal expert who is the founder and director of Massachusetts Paranormal Crossroads, says that there are many long-standing stories that John Pickering Putnam was an amateur occultist and that Charlesgate Hall was "designed and built with the right materials to act as a magnet for the paranormal."

Boston University bought the building in 1947 and quickly put it to use as a female dormitory for the school. Word passed around the school quickly about the building's bad energy, some even going so far as to claim that the negative forces inside the dorm would drive people to suicide. Cold spots were common, and alarm clocks around the building would go off at 6:11 a.m. regardless of what time they had actually been set for.

Six seems to be an unlucky number at Charlesgate Hall. Three girls who lived in the building during its time as a Boston University dorm said that their sixth-floor room had a closet none of them would use. Each girl, independent of the others, would touch the doorknob and then slowly back away. Later, they were told that someone had hanged themselves in the closet during its time as an apartment building.

While claims of suicides that lead to hauntings are rife in college urban legends, Charlesgate Hall actually has some evidence to back up the story. A March 15, 1908 edition of the *Boston Globe* reported on the death of a resident at the Charlesgate by his own hand.

"Despondent and worn out by insomnia, and apparently for no other reason than melancholy [depression] induced by his nervous trouble, Westwood T—, junior partner of '—' & Son, manufacturers of shoe bindings at 40 Oliver St, shot himself in his apartment in the Charlesgate hotel early yesterday morning," began the *Globe* article.

Westwood was dedicated in his aim to kill himself. While his wife slept in the other room, he hung up a mirror so he could carefully watch his aim and then shot himself in the head. His wife, awakened by the noise, walked into the bedroom next door and found Westwood's body half inside the closet, his hand still wrapped tightly around the revolver he had used to take his own life. The medical examiner quickly ruled the case a suicide, just one of several that are reported to have taken place at the Charlesgate over the building's lifetime.

The suicide of Westwood T. might also be linked to another haunting that was reported at Charlesgate Hall during its time as a Boston University

Left: Larger than many of the other buildings around it, the Charlesgate sometimes feels like it's looming over passersby.

dorm. One student, again on the sixth floor, awoke to find the spirit of a man hovering very close above him as he slept. The student, now fully awake, couldn't seem to move his arms or legs to get away from the ghost. The student began to struggle with the spirit. Several other students, and a resident assistant who lived on that floor, were drawn to the room once the student began to scream for help. The other students also witnessed the ghost. Still, the arrival of the others seemed to break the ghost's hold on the student. Once he was able to hop out of bed, the spirit disappeared entirely. The student refused to sleep in the room again, and allegedly the school closed the room off from further use by anyone else until it was sold in 1972.

If the hovering ghost wasn't that of Westwood, ironically, it might have been that of the building's creator. John Pickering Putnam is on the long list of people who have died at the Charlesgate over the years. Contemporary records don't indicate how he perished, but the *Boston Globe* reported the death of the famed architect inside the building on February 24, 1917, at the age of sixty.

While Boston University students may have had some juicy ghost stories to tell during their time at the Charlesgate, nothing compares to the happenings that occurred while Emerson College owned the building. This was during the 1980s and '90s, when, of all things, Ouija board fever gripped the Emerson College population. Spurred on by the ghost stories, many Charlesgate Hall residents gathered together friends to try and communicate with the spirits that were rumored to plague their building.

One girl's impromptu séance was interrupted by the frantic ringing of her phone. It was her dad, begging her to stop whatever she was doing at that moment. The girl had never mentioned the ghost stories, or her newly bought Ouija board, to her parents, but the first night she opened the box to the "game," her father was gripped with a sense of dread and felt compelled to reach out to her. The incident disturbed the student enough that she kept her promise to her father to never use a Ouija board within the confines of Charlesgate Hall again.

Another group of Emerson College students playing with a Ouija board were said to have stirred up something malignant that continued to target one of the students long after the board was put away. Further rounds with the Ouija board saw this dark force compulsively spelling out the student's name and making threats against him. One night, while this student was showering, his roommate brought the board out again. The same dark presence arrived and kept spelling out "Ha, ha." When asked what the

This beautiful Romanesque Revival building was once used as a dormitory for two different Boston colleges.

spirit found so funny, the only reply they got was: "AC, DC, AC, DC." The participants couldn't figure out what the spirit meant until the roommate came back from the shower, shaking and pale.

As soon as the student turned the water on and was just about to step into the shower, he told the group, the light above him began to flicker. He could see that the light bulb was loose, though it had been fine until just a second previous. Not thinking, he began to reach up to screw the light bulb in tighter. At the last second, he looked down and realized he was standing in a pool of water, which would have greatly increased his risk of electrocution. The student was sure the spirit had been trying to live up to its threats and harm him.

Eventually, Emerson College banned the use of Ouija boards at Charlesgate Hall. They said the game was getting out of hand and leading to too many disturbances among the residents. Many students felt the school knew the boards were stirring up forces in the old building and didn't want to admit to all the problems that had been reported that were unexplainable. There were even rumors of a secret "Charlesgate File," where school administrators tucked away every inexplicable occurrence that was reported to them. Then, of course, came further tales of some sort of paranormal investigator who was hired by Emerson College to quietly assess the reports hidden away in the secret file.

Even with the Ouija boards put, presumably, to rest, students still made lots of reports of strange activity in Charlesgate Hall. A man in black was most often mentioned. Other students complained of bad vibes, sleep disturbances, sleepwalking and objects moving across tables or through the air, and several even swore they had their blankets ripped from them as they lay in bed in otherwise empty rooms.

Since Charlesgate Hall went through its latest incarnation as a luxury condo building, the reports of ghost stories have stopped abruptly. Either the ghosts like the condo owners better than they liked living with college students and have fallen quiet or the new owners aren't willing to damage their property values by talking about waking up blanketless in freezing cold rooms.

EMERSON COLLEGE

BOSTON

The Cutler Majestic Theater didn't start off as part of a college. Built in 1903, the theater combined classic styling with the most up-to-date technological advances of the time—namely the 4,500 light bulbs scattered throughout its lobby and main stage area. Originally, it was an opera house, but by the time the 1920s rolled around, the theater was born again as a vaudeville hotspot. It was the first of several incarnations the theater would go through. In the 1950s, it became a movie theater and somehow managed to struggle along for the next thirty years until it was bought by Emerson College.

Emerson College would revitalize the theater. Renovations to the 1,200-seat building would be an ongoing process for the school over the next twenty years. Eventually, the layers of paint that had accumulated would be stripped off, and the beautiful Beaux-Arts architecture that had been commissioned by the theater's original owner, Eben Dyer Jordan of the Jordan Marsh department store dynasty, would be restored. Opera would return to the theater's stage, along with many other productions, professional and student led, each year.

The Cutler Majestic Theater is listed on both the National Register of Historic Places and the Massachusetts Register of Historic Places. It also holds the title of Boston's second-oldest theater. But it may take the number one spot for haunted theater, which in Boston is saying quite a lot.

One of the longest-standing ghost stories about the Cutler Majestic Theater concerns a former Boston mayor who died during a show and isn't willing to give up his favorite seat even after death. Much of the tale smacks

Right: The Cutler Majestic Theater began life as an opera house. Today, it serves as home to a variety of theatrical and musical performances.

of urban legend, but a few sources have pegged George Albee Hibbard as the mythical mayor. Hibbard began his political career as postmaster for the city of Boston. In 1908, he would be elected mayor and would become famous for starting a commission to investigate city government spending. George Hibbard's love of the theater is well documented, though no contemporary sources mention if he died there.

After Hibbard's death, his wife would become an actress. Ironically, she debuted at the Cutler Majestic Theater. Some sources say that's the real reason why Hibbard's ghost still haunts his favorite chair. But whether he stayed around to applaud his wife's new career or to keep a ghostly eye on what she was getting up to after his death is cause for debate. Acting wasn't the most respectable job for a woman of her time, and in her first role, Hibbard's wife is said to have played a cigar-smoking showgirl with a love of fast cars and expensive diamonds.

Also in the audience of the Majestic is the spirit of a little girl. She roams the aisles during some performances, begging for little treats or candy. But whoever the girl is, she's a shy spook. People say that if they look directly at her or try to speak to her, she disappears as if she were never there.

The theater's spirit hotspot is the third-floor balcony. This section of the theater is often closed off for what is said to be safety concerns. Many hold firm to the belief that the balcony is kept closed off to visitors in the hopes that people won't realize just how haunted it really is.

The balcony's most famous ghosts are a couple dressed in what is described as Edwardian-era clothing. Long after death, the couple is still firmly in love. They dance and twirl around the balcony, stopping periodically to flip down seats so they can sit and watch the performances. Superstition at the Cutler Majestic Theater says the couple will watch only the best shows, and it is considered a huge compliment to the cast if anyone reports seeing the couple during their show. But the afterlife isn't all dancing and shows for this couple. A few witnesses have seen them fighting angrily and pushing each other around, leading to speculation about just how it was that this fiery, temperamental couple died and came to haunt the theater.

Flipped-down seats run rampant in this area of the Majestic Theater, but they're not all credited to the spectral couple. Historically, this area was set aside for minorities and those who could afford only the cheapest seats. A long-standing legend about the theater is that a terrible accident occurred there shortly after the theater opened and that most of the ghosts date from this time. A couple of young men, climbing around the grid holding the lights, are said to have gotten the idea to pull a prank during one sold-out show. They snipped what they thought were the wires to some of the main stage's lights, hoping to plunge the theater into darkness and the crowd into disarray. Instead, a group of lights came crashing down on the audience, killing several in the third-floor area.

Whether the story has any historical fact is hard to confirm. But many have seen the impressions of invisible bodies sitting down in the empty flipped-over seats as if unseen people were sitting there enjoying the show. Students at Emerson College have come to terms with their ghosts. Upperclassmen are quick to teach the incoming freshman to say, "Excuse me" as they pass by the flipped down seats—they'd hate to offend their resident ghosts!

The Majestic Theater is home to many more unexplained phenomena. Students who have held productions in the theater tell stories of disconcerting noises and unexplainable power disruptions. There seems to be at least one ghostly presence in the sound room that is credited with turning off equipment of the shows he doesn't like. The slightest blip in the sound equipment is considered to be a bad review from the theater's sound room ghost.

Chillingly, the backstage area has one room that has become known as the nightmare room. Students complain of having extreme claustrophobic responses when they are inside of it that are far out of line with the actual size of the room. The smothering energy of the room has created feelings of choking in more physically sensitive students. Others say they feel nothing at all when entering the room. The nightmare room is thought to be a kind of dead spot that either kills emotions or makes you feel as though you might be killed as the air is slowly squeezed from your lungs by a strong grip.

EMMANUEL COLLEGE

BOSTON

E mmanuel College is a co-ed Roman Catholic liberal arts college located in Boston's Longwood medical neighborhood, but the many ghost stories told around campus date back to the school's days as a women's college. Of course, this is not surprising considering that the school began in 1919 and went coeducational only as recently as 2001.

School legends say that the ghost in St. Joseph's Hall is that of a former student who lingers on after dying before she could complete her education.

St. Joseph's Hall is the site of an unusual bathroom haunting. The spirit—that of a young woman—manifests in the mirrors of a second-floor lavatory. Students washing up in front of the mirrors see the image of the young girl, her long hair dripping wet and a sad expression on her face, stepping out of the showers behind them. When they turn to look, there is no one there. Even visitors to the St. Joseph Hall dorm, having never heard the legend of the ghost, have reported seeing her.

Popular legend around the Emmanuel campus says the ghostly girl was once a student at the college and that she died without warning after a lingering illness. She still haunts the campus because she feels that her education is unfinished business that she must complete before she can pass on. No one has attempted to explain why she's seen only in the dormitory bathroom and not in any of the classrooms.

Resident assistants in St. Joseph's have had problems in their rooms unrelated to the bathroom spirit. Several RAs have reported returning to their carefully locked rooms to find windows opened, faucets in their private bathrooms running and their belongings moved to interesting new positions. Nothing of value has ever been reported stolen, and the rooms don't appear to have been broken into. This has led many students to think the activity in the rooms has more to do with a mischievous spirit than with an ineffectual burglar.

St. James, now a dormitory attached to the main administration building on campus, was once housing for the nuns who worked at the school. The buildings have a long history of unwanted visitors, though the living kinds have been more of a problem for Emmanuel College than the dead ones. At one point, a homeless man was discovered living in the bell tower attached to the administration building. He had, it seemed, been living there for a significant amount of time, somehow unseen by students or staff. It raised a minor brouhaha at the school that Emmanuel College has gone out of its way to try and live down.

The fourth floor of St. James had gone unused for many of the years it was a home for the nuns of Emmanuel College; that is, unused by the nuns perhaps, but not entirely empty. Students often saw a man's face peering down at the campus from the fourth-floor windows of St. James. The lesson of the homeless man living Hunchback of Notre Dame style in the bell tower has not been easily forgotten, and students have become much quicker to contact campus security whenever they see something suspicious. However, no one has ever been caught prowling around the

Emmanuel College is located across many buildings in Boston's Longwood medical neighborhood.

building, let alone on the fourth floor, when students have reported seeing the face spying down at them.

The administration building attached to St. James has a ghost of its own. One spring break, a security guard reported seeing a young woman in old-fashioned clothing walking down the main staircase of the building. Besides the fact that it was the middle of the night, and during spring break to boot, the girl gave off an eerie vibe that raised goose bumps on the security guard's arms. He called out to the girl, demanding she say who she was and what she was doing there, but she took no notice of him.

Ignoring his fear, the security guard dashed up the stairs toward her. The girl casually turned and walked into an alcove near the stairs. The guard dashed in after her and found the alcove empty. She didn't pass him on the stairs, and there was no exit leading from the alcove. He never figured out where she had gone, and he never saw her again.

ENDICOTT COLLEGE

BEVERLY

E ndicott College is a 235-acre four-year private college located in Beverly, Massachusetts, in the heart of the North Shore. The college was begun in 1939 and was plagued almost immediately by ghost stories. Tracing back stories associated with the land where the school is located brings up even more ghostly bits of folklore. Old maps of the area call this part of Beverly the Witch's Woods, as it was long rumored that many escaped being accused in the Salem Witch Trials by hiding out in the dense forests that were located here, and warns that the woods were haunted by many spirits. Endicott College boasts at least five different haunted locations on campus, while the town of Beverly features several haunts of its own that are located near the sprawling oceanfront school.

Winthrop Hall, a seaside mansion built in 1845 by John Thissell, is the site of an absolutely classic New England ghost story if there ever was one. The house, once used as a home for the college president and now a residence hall for some of the school's nearly five thousand students, features a prominent widow's walk along its top floor. Old wives' tales have long said

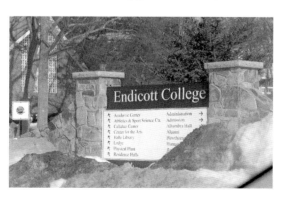

The Endicott College campus is a unique mix of ultramodern buildings and historic old mansions.

these railed platforms were created during the height of the age of sail so the wives of mariners could easily watch the sea in hopes of their husbands' safe return. Less romantic architects and historians have said the popular widow's walk was more of a natural evolution of the cupola and that they were used more to ease the battle of a chimney fire than to ease the minds of sailors' worried wives. An equally popular legend about widow's walks is that more than a few grief-stricken young widows were known to have thrown themselves off the platforms when they learned their husbands had perished at sea. The story about Winthrop Hall's ghost is a classic form of this type of ghostly legend.

The story says that the young wife of a sea captain spent months lighting candles in the windows of the building that is now known as Winthrop Hall in the hopes of guiding her husband safely home from sea. Upon learning he had been lost to a shipwreck, the young widow committed suicide by throwing herself from the very walk she had paced so many nights hoping to see his safe return. At the moment of her death, her outpouring of grief was so strong that it flipped the paintings in the home upside down.

To students at Endicott College, the young woman of this legend is known as the "pink lady" due to a flowing rose-colored gown she is most often seen wearing. The spirit of the pink lady is said to roam the hallways of Winthrop Hall and has also been reported wandering outside the house along the edge of the sea. There is a long-standing tradition among the students that if you light candles in the windows of Winthrop Hall, you'll find a historic painting in the building's foyer flipped over, just as it was said to have done the night of the pink lady's death.

Other versions of the pink lady's tale do away with the widow's walk completely. In the second version of her story, she is said to have hanged herself in one of the mansion's upstairs rooms, not to have leaped to her death from the walk. Students who have roomed in this particular dorm say that the doors never stay closed tightly and that they slam open and shut at will as if moved by an unseen hand. Chillingly, other students have reported finding seaweed draped among the building's fire escapes on the nights that the foyer painting is found flipped upside down. Whether the seaweed is a manifestation of the pink lady or of nightly visits from her drowned sea captain husband dredged up from the ocean floor and hoping to return to her side once again remains open to spine-chilling speculation.

While the legend of the pink lady may sound like just that—nothing more than a popular story to tell around campus—many college administrators have come forward over the years to admit to their own encounters with the spirit. It's one thing when a student claims to have seen a ghost and quite another when a staff or faculty member is willing to state publically that he or she has as well!

The earliest known case of this comes from none other than Endicott College founder Eleanor Tupper, PhD. Tupper served as president of the school she founded for many years. In 1985, she would write *Endicott and I*, a book about her time at the college. The ghost of Winthrop Hall makes an appearance in this book.

Dr. Tupper says in *Endicott and I* that while every year students would claim to have had uncanny experiences with the pink lady (though in her book, Dr. Tupper calls her the "blue lady"), she never gave the stories much credence herself until her seven-year-old daughter, Priscilla, came to her in a fright. Priscilla said that she had been approached by a beautiful woman who had no legs and had hovered ever closer to her while she was playing outside Winthrop Hall. Dr. Tupper said the rumors about the ghost had purposely been kept from her young daughter and that the child had never expressed any interest in scary tales, yet she was able to describe in perfect detail the same sort of figure that students had been reporting to Dr. Tupper for years.

Perhaps it is because Dr. Tupper, a religious woman with a reputation for being professional and completely no nonsense, was so open about her family's experience with the ghost that other staff members have felt free to admit to their own encounters. Liz Atilano, current director of Endicott College's Career Center and former resident director of Winthrop Hall, has shared her ghost stories with several different sources over the years.

"It wasn't like the movies," Atilano told the authors of *Real-Life Stories of Supernatural Experiences* in 2003. "There were no moans and groans. She was never scary. I think she was there to welcome us."

Other credible eyewitnesses to the pink lady haunting include a former Beverly police officer, former dean of students Sally King, a former college registrar who worked at the school at the same time as King and the college's director of student development.

Even historical accounts add their voices to the layers of evidence that something strange has been going on at Winthrop Hall for a very long time. The Endicott College archives contain a story from the daughter of one of Winthrop Hall's early owners that recounts her experience of getting lost on the property that would later become Endicott College. The girl, daughter of John King, accompanied by a cousin and her maid, became lost in the woods after a picnic despite her familiarity with the land surrounding her longtime home. After walking for several hours, the three young women saw a colonial farmhouse in a clearing before them. The three women rushed toward the house—one none had ever seen before though they had lived in the area their entire lives—to get directions that would take them home. But every time they approached the old house, it would disappear. When they finally did make their way home, they asked everyone they could find about the strange house. No one else in town recognized it. But because the King family was so well respected by their neighbors, most believed the story and chalked it up as just another odd occurrence in Witch's Woods.

Interestingly, Winthrop Hall has another more obscure ghostly connection than that of its popular legendary pink lady and her long-lost sea captain. Historically, there is evidence that the home was once a stop on the Underground Railroad that helped bring slaves from southern plantations up to Canada, where they could live as free men and women. And just behind Winthrop Hall, on Mingo Beach, there are stories of the ghost of a former slave. In fact, Mingo Beach is named for the slave Robin Mingo. The story goes that in the 1700s, Mingo was promised his freedom by his master, Thomas Woodbery, if the tide along that stretch of Massachusetts coast ever dropped low enough that Mingo could walk on dry land to a distant rock that could just barely be seen jutting from the choppy ocean waves.

The most popular versions of this story say that Mingo died in the attempt or that he spent his life waiting for the tide to drop but that the event didn't take place until just days after the slave died from old age. The First Parish Church in Beverly has records of Robin Mingo's life and gives us a much different, and much happier, ending to his story. Church documents agree that the fabled deal between the slave and his master was made but that Mingo, thanks to a full moon that resulted in an extremely low tide, was able to walk out to the agreed upon rock without so much as dampening the soles of his shoes. Thomas Woodbery was true to his word and not only granted Mingo his freedom but also deeded him, in exchange for twenty-six shillings, a small plot of land directly on the beach. While the people of the time wouldn't have thought it was much of a deal, as farming so close to the ocean wouldn't be profitable, Mingo built a fine house for himself and his Native American wife on Mingo Beach, and they enjoyed lovely ocean views, if not plentiful crops, for the rest of their lives. After his death in 1748, people began to report seeing his ghost wandering the beach that eventually came to bear his name.

Among Endicott College's other popular ghost stories is that of Julie, whose ghost is often reported in Brindle Hall. Unlike Winthrop Hall, Brindle Hall is no historic mansion by the sea with a long history of owners to lend credence to its ghost stories. Brindle Hall was built in 1963 and was known as East Hall until 1993, when it was renamed in honor of Edward Brindle, a former Endicott College vice-president of business affairs. Today, it is used as one of two freshman dorms. Julie, according to the stories, was once a resident in the building back during its days as East Hall. She was a fan of marbles—so much so that her ghost is still associated with them. The sound of marbles rolling or being slowly dropped on the ground has kept more than one Endicott College freshman awake at night, and Julie has been blamed for this, and many other, disturbances. Other common occurrences in Brindle Hall that are credited to Julie's ghost are the sound of knocking in the walls or on bed headboards, handprints that mysteriously appear on the glass windows on the upper floors of the buildings and the clickity-clacking of computer keyboards by invisible hands.

Many claim to see the name "Julie" spelled out by the skeletal branches of winter trees located directly outside the building. But just who exactly Julie was is something of a mystery. It is sometimes said that she was a student who disappeared from the college under mysterious circumstances back when the building was still fairly new. Julie's well-known love of marbles seems to lend some support to this idea. While marbles are a classic toy believed to have been played in some form or another dating back to prehistoric times, the New England states saw something of a regional marble craze in the late 1960s and early '70s. It was during these years that a variation of the classic game that involved using one's feet instead of hands, which is said to have been created in the Nashua, New Hampshire area of New England, reignited the toy's popularity among players of many ages for a brief few years.

Other times, it has been said that she was a student at Endicott College in the late 1980s who committed suicide in her dorm room one night. Current-day students have even pinpointed the site of Julie's supposed suicide room: 314. And whatever the truth is about who Julie was and what went on in that room, number 314 does seem to have greater than average reports of ghostly activity in a building that seems to be extraordinarily haunted to begin with. In and around the room, several people have reported feeling physically touched or even pushed by unseen hands. And while Julie is generally considered to be a benign spirit, the one thing everyone agrees on is that she doesn't like people not believing in her. Students who have scoffed at the idea that they might be living with a marble-loving ghost have reported books flying off shelves and even light bulbs exploding in what would seem to be some kind of ghostly temper tantrum.

Not to be outdone by Winthrop Hall or Brindle Hall, another of Endicott College's dorms, Reynolds Hall, also has a ghost in residence. Reynolds Hall was the first building to be put to use by Endicott College when it was founded in 1939. Originally built as a summer home for a Boston banker, the house was sold in 1921 and became the Kendall Hall School for Girls. Eventually, the Kendall Hall School would be moved to Peterborough, New Hampshire, and the building would sit empty for several years before becoming the start of Endicott College. The ghost that lingers there to this day seems to date from the building's time as a girls' school.

The ghost is that of a little girl; many say she is only five or six years old. Luckily, however, she ended up in Reynolds Hall. She's a playful spirit and not a melancholy one. She is known for tapping out clumsy tunes on the hall's piano, playing with window shades and rolling balls around the wood floors. Some students have even seen the spirit, never directly, but she is very clear when reflected in mirrors.

If there's one place on the Endicott College campus that should be haunted just based on looks alone, College Hall would have to be that place. Bought in

Reports of ghosts in College Hall have dropped off since the building has been converted from classroom to administrative use.

the 1940s from the estate of William Amory Gardner, College Hall is made of gray stone and looks vaguely castle like in its silhouette. The building is currently used for administration purposes. Previously, it has been used for both classroom space and a residence building. Few contemporary stories of College Hall's ghosts are told today, but back when it was a series of classrooms, it was well known among students as a place of paranormal happenings.

At that time, the rumor was that a former servant of the Gardner family was still hard at work in College Hall. Chalkboards left overnight would be cleaned spotlessly by morning even though no one could ever find a maintenance worker who would take credit for the careful cleaning. Books would be found rearranged on the bookshelves or moved into other classrooms entirely. For that matter, furniture had a habit of traveling from room to room at night when the building was supposed to be empty.

Whoever the ghostly cleaner was, he kept his activities solely to the classrooms of College Hall. Students who lived there during its time as a dormitory had to pick up after themselves and arrange their own furniture.

"The Halle Library ghost was so active I used to say that we should issue him a library card," jokes Claire, a former Endicott College library aid. "But no one else realized that I was being serious when I said it."

The Halle Library has a dedicated reader wandering the stacks.

Nobody warned Claire that the library might be haunted before she started working at the Halle Library. But that's not surprising considering how quiet people tend to be about this ghost. Places like College Hall just look so much more like they should be haunted, and Winthrop House has so much history surrounding it, everyone just knows it must be haunted. Halle Library has a much less mysterious air about it and a, sad to say, more or less boring ghost.

Claire, who says she would see the ghost from time to time, described him as an older man, a little chubby, whom she usually saw sitting in one of the library's reading chairs. The first time she came across him, she didn't even realize she was seeing something no one else around her was seeing. Forget about whatever idea you have of a misty apparition growing slowly more transparent as the terrified witness watches it. This spirit was so fully formed that it wasn't until Claire saw him in the same clothing in the same chair on several different occasions that she realized she was seeing a ghost.

No one knows who the man was in life. But it's a safe bet that he was a reader. The ghost's chair would often be found with a stack of several books, one usually still open part way, as if it had been put down mid-read, resting beside it. Claire got in the habit of putting the closed books away and leaving the unfinished one sitting near the chair.

While most people do not seem to be sensitive enough to see the apparition, many others have felt his presence. Readers wandering the stacks report feeling as if someone is standing directly behind them browsing books over their shoulders, and some say the ghost has helped them find the right book in times of trouble.

When a mishelved book stumped one frantic Endicott College senior who needed it for a paper that was due the next day, she was stunned to hear a loud thump directly behind her in the stacks. Turning the corner to the next row of shelves, she felt a random cold spot and noticed a book lying on the floor as if it had been pushed from its shelf. It was, of course, the very book she'd been looking for, though there had been no one anywhere near her in the library to take credit for knocking it off the shelf.

FRAMINGHAM STATE UNIVERSITY

FRAMINGHAM

During his life, Horace Mann played a vital role in education, not just in the state of Massachusetts but also across the entire United States, as well as founding the institution that would eventually become Framingham State University. Born in 1796, Mann would go on to serve in the Massachusetts House of Representatives, the Massachusetts Senate and the United States House of Representatives. In between his terms in the state senate and the U.S. House of Representatives, Horace Mann served as secretary of the Massachusetts State Board of Education, the first of its kind in the entire nation. Mann was a huge proponent of the idea that universal education would lead to a disciplined workforce of responsible citizens. To this end, he established a system of "normal schools" tasked with establishing teaching norms that would train teachers to having a universally held standard of education.

Mann's first normal school was created in Lexington, Massachusetts, in 1839. Mann placed Cyrus Peirce, a Unitarian minister and educator, at its head as president. This normal school would go through several locational moves and name changes, eventually evolving into the organization we now know as Framingham State University.

The university still offers teaching degrees, along with a whole host of other disciplines, to its close to ten thousand students annually. Fifteen hundred of those students choose to live on the seventy-three-acre Framingham University campus. Two of the residency buildings on campus are Horace Mann Hall and Peirce Hall, named, of course, in honor of Horace Mann and Cyrus Peirce, respectively.

Both of these buildings have been the sites of unexplained, and unexplainable, phenomena over the years. One interesting feature of these buildings is the underground tunnel that connects them to each other and to several other nearby buildings. These kinds of tunnels were a fairly common addition to college campuses in Massachusetts at one point, the idea being that students would be able to move easily between buildings regardless of the weather, but they have largely fallen into disuse. The University of Massachusetts–Lowell campus still uses some of its tunnels, but as a whole, on other college campuses they tend to be long rumored—and long sealed off. Framingham State University's tunnels have been abandoned for some time, but many students claim they are still accessible if you know the right place to go. College legend says that the wiring in the tunnels was faulty, causing a fire that killed one student, and that it was then that the college discontinued their use.

You'll find plenty of students who say that the tunnels are haunted and that the activity going on down there sometimes spills into Horace Mann Hall and Peirce Hall. But either because the tunnels aren't nearly as easy to get into as university rumors promise or out of fear of being reprimanded for their clandestine explorations, you'll have a hard time finding students who will admit to experiencing the tunnel haunting firsthand.

Horace Mann Hall, which sits directly over the former foundation of a much earlier building, seems to be the more haunted of the two dormitories that are named after early college founders Horace Mann and Cyrus Peirce. It has more reported incidents and a wider variety of phenomena reported. Sadly, these all tend to run the usual gamut as any other mildly haunted house. Horace Mann Hall has the prerequisite cold spots, strange noises and knockings and unexplained sounds of voices and laughter coming from otherwise empty rooms.

The one way that Horace Mann Hall really stands out as a haunted place is in the prevalence of orb photographs taken in and around the building. Not sure what an orb photo is or if you've ever taken one? Most people, at one point or another, have seen some form of an orb photograph in their lives, even if they didn't know what they were seeing. The "orb" that gives the phenomenon its name is usually a fuzzy or misty-looking globe seen floating in photographs. They come in a variety of sizes and in color tend to be white, though you will find orbs more rarely in all shades of the color spectrum or even just partially tinged with color. These are semitransparent circles that are not seen with the naked eye at the time the photograph is taken; rather, they appear afterward, only in the photo itself. Orb photographs may feature just one or two of the fuzzy spots, or if you're lucky, the photograph may capture the image of hundreds of them.

For true-life ghost story aficionados, orb photographs are believed to be a kind of evidence of a haunting taking place. While some believe that auras of living people can produce the orb image in a photograph, it is generally accepted among the paranormal community that the orbs seen are the energy or souls of the departed. Think of them as the visual equivalent of a cold spot. While the common belief seems to be that a "ghost photograph" shows a misty-looking, Victorian-clad figure floating down the stairs, these types of photos are extremely, extremely rare. The most common kind of ghost photograph anyone will ever take will show nothing more than orbs. Most people, no matter how many haunted locations they visit and how many photos they take, will never get anything more than an orb photograph. The good news is that if they want to take orb photographs, chances are they'll end up with thousands of them.

If orb photography is proof for the true believers, for the skeptical among us, orb photography is evidence of absolutely nothing more than dust on the lens of the camera. Orbs can easily be created, on purpose, using anything from a fine mist of water, to pollen, to powders, to dust. The ease in creating the type of backscatter necessary to make an orb photograph has called the entire idea of them being any sort of evidence of ghostly activity into question. Even those who are full-fledged believers in the afterlife admit that orb photography can be one of the most easily mistaken, and most easily faked, kind of corroboration of a haunting. It doesn't help that so many people go ghost hunting in absolute wrecks of buildings; that is, the very places that are prime locations to end up with a dusty camera lens.

So while the huge amount of orb photographs taken at Horace Mann Hall is certainly tantalizing, it is not, in and of itself, the kind of proof most people want when they're trying to make up their minds about whether a building is haunted or not. But if you're not looking for proof, or want nothing more than to simply confirm your suspicions for yourself, pick up a camera and head over to Horace Mann Hall. If you feel any cold spots or just get the feeling that something is sharing a room with you that you can't see, start clicking. You might be surprised by what shows up in the photographs.

Peirce Hall doesn't get nearly as many reports of odd occurrences as Horace Mann Hall. And you probably won't get many, if any, orb photographs if you go here to do a little ghost hunting. But it does have a slightly more unusual phenomenon that's fascinating in and of itself. People, such as resident assistants who have a reason to be sleeping alone in the building before the rest of the student population moves in, have found that whatever is haunting Peirce Hall doesn't care for vanity.

Go to bed in Peirce Hall, and in the morning you'll find the building's ghost was busy all night long moving mirrors out of rooms and piling them up, reflective side to the wall, in the hallways. It's ironic considering the long history mirrors have had with ghosts, divination and other occult arts. As you'll see in other chapters in this book, many ghosts manifest themselves in mirrors. A ghost that goes out of its way to shield itself from mirrors is a fairly unique occurrence.

HARVARD UNIVERSITY

CAMBRIDGE

Yes, it's true. Not even the hallowed halls of Harvard University are free from ghostly activity. The world-famous Ivy League school was founded in 1636, making it both the oldest university and the oldest corporation in the United States. It began with the mission of educating Congregationalist and Unitarian clergy. The scope of the school's offerings has certainly changed a lot in the nearly four hundred years since its founding.

Famous Harvard alumni include Microsoft founder Bill Gates, Henry David Thoreau of *Walden* fame, transcendentalist Ralph Waldo Emerson, poet T.S. Eliot, cellist Yo-Yo Ma, comedian Conan O'Brien, actress Natalie Portman, basketball player Jeremy Lin, Facebook creator Mark Zuckerberg and Unabomber Ted Kaczynski. In all, more than seven United States presidents have been Harvard University graduates, and more than forty current and former faculty have been Nobel Laureates.

Despite the prestige of the school, Thayer Hall, now Harvard's largest freshman dormitory, began life as a textile mill. But even though it's been put into longtime use as a residence hall, many of the original millworkers are still showing up for their shifts each night. These Victorian-clad ghosts go about their business, seemingly unaware of the building's more current occupants. They walk along hallways that no longer exist and pass through walls that have sprung up where doorways existed in their own times.

While both a writer at HauntedHills.com and paranormal researcher Fiona Broome were contacted by a Harvard professor who wanted to share his story of the Thayer Hall ghosts, some Harvard University students are a bit more cynical about the legend.

"I have seen no evidence to that so far," Josh A. Bookin, a skeptical Thayer proctor, told the *Harvard Crimson* in 2009 when he was asked about the ghosts. "The most notable of the out-of-the-ordinary activities are parties that need to be broken up."

But Bookin did go on to add that if he ever did have a run-in with any of the building's former occupants, he'd have a different reaction than most: "I'm not going to do the whole, 'Dude, run!' thing. I don't get scared of ghosts. I'm interested in the stories that ghosts can provide about history."

Bookin should have tried standing outside Thayer Hall during a brightly lit winter night. Over the years, dozens upon dozens of students have reported seeing long queues of ghosts in period clothing lining up outside the building's entrances, trying to get in. These incidences are most often reported at night and during times of cold, wintry weather.

While Thayer Hall has a plethora of ghosts, the other freshman dormitory at Harvard University, Massachusetts Hall, can boast only one. It seems surprising for a building that was created all the way back in 1718, making it the oldest surviving building at Harvard and the oldest dormitory in the country, that it hasn't yet collected a wild gang of haunts. But this lone ghost is active enough that even former assistant dean of freshmen William C. Young is said to have publically expressed his own belief in the spirit during his tenure at the school.

Many students describe their time at Harvard University as the best years of their lives. One student loves the school so much that he's hung around well into death, returning to his dorm room at Massachusetts Hall every fall since the early 1900s. The Harvard stories say that he is Holbrook Smith, a member of the class of 1914. Fitted in his old-fashioned garb, he is a startling sight for the many students who stumble across him wandering the hallways. William C. Young is supposed to have seen and interacted with the spirit at one time. When Young was assistant dean of freshmen, he saw the famed ghost and promptly asked him to leave.

"You've ruined a perfectly good thing," the ghost was supposed to have said as it faded away.

It was assumed at the time that the spirit would leave the campus for good. But it was a bit of misdirection on the ghost's part. Young never saw the spirit again, but lots of other people continue to—to this day.

In all, Holbrook is a pretty boring spirit, although it would seem that he is an unusually powerful one. In the 1970s, a noted psychic came to speak at

Massachusetts Hall. In the psychic's opening remarks, she warned students not to bother trying to take her picture. The medium told the students that she could see the ghostly alumni in the audience and that his unnaturally strong energy would render their cameras useless. Of course, this only encouraged students to take more pictures than they originally would have. Reportedly, each photograph from each camera came out completely black.

Weld Hall is another old Harvard University building finding new use as a dorm. Built in 1870, it's not nearly as old as Massachusetts Hall, but the lovely Queen Anne–style dorm does have a kind of haunted air about it. The funny thing about the ghosts in this Victorian-era building is that they didn't start popping up until the 1960s.

It was during the 1960s that a major renovation of Weld Hall was undertaken. While the building had never had any reports of paranormal activity before this project was started, the construction and changes made seemed to have stirred up some strange energy that is still active even today. Students have been reporting feeling watched and followed, finding personal items moved from locked places and noises that occur without an earthly source since the 1960 renovations.

In 1985, a group of Harvard University students went so far as to hold an impromptu séance in their Weld Hall room in hopes of contacting the building's spirits. Sitting around a red candle, the roommates were somehow able to conjure up an apparition. It was that of an old woman with long gray hair and wearing a dark cloak. She said nothing, just watched the girls while leaning casually against their dorm room wall, and eventually she faded away into a cold mist.

The ghost's features were very hard to make out, and she was unable to communicate with the girls even when they were, presumably, doing everything in their power to be receptive to hearing her. This suggests a rather weak spirit that doesn't have enough energy to do much more than flicker lights or make some odd noises in the walls.

University Hall has not just one ghost but a textile mill full of them. This Harvard University building is the site of a ghostly dinner party that has been reported for one hundred years or more. The beautiful white granite building is on the National Register of Historic Places and has an interesting history of its own outside of the ghostly dinner party.

The building was created by Charles Bulfinch, the architect behind such famous buildings as the Maine Statehouse, the Massachusetts General Hospital and the intermediate United States Capitol rotunda and dome. While the pedigree of the building is unimpeachable, the white Chelmsford granite that gives University Hall its clean and classic exterior was cut by prisoners at Charlestown Prison, not so far away from Harvard University in distance but legions away in terms of its place in society. Originally, the building housed the campus dining room, and two stories of it were dedicated to a chapel. Both of these were gone by 1867, carved up and partitioned off into classrooms. Little else is notable about the building beyond its beginnings, with the exception of a 1969 protest over Harvard University's public stance on the war in Vietnam that saw students take over the building for eighteen hours. The standoff ended more or less peacefully when Massachusetts state troopers were called in to remove the students from the building.

The protest may have left no echoes to rumble around the white halls, but there's been a dinner party of some kind going on for ages. Standing at the southwest entrance of the building, students swear you can hear the clinking of utensils against plates and voices murmuring in friendly conversation while they eat. Considering the building's one-time use as a dining hall, one can only assume the ghosts date back to the very first years the building was on campus.

There was once another ghost that was well known to those who spent time around University Hall but has passed on to a hopefully better place. A large pine tree once stood at the northeast corner of the building for many years and seemed to be the center of a haunting. The spirit of a young girl was often seen under or around the tree. Unlike many ghosts, which merely make themselves known with a feeling or a waft of cold air, she was a full apparition, fully visible to anyone who reported her presence. In time, the tree needed to be cut down. Once it was removed, the ghostly young woman was never seen again. Who she was or why she had such strong ties to the tree remain unknown.

A fairly unique feature at Harvard University is the school's use of "houses." This is much more common abroad than in the United States. The idea of houses is familiar to most Americans only in recent years thanks to the popularity of the Harry Potter series. Generations of kids who grow up wishing they had a round with the sorting hat to find out if they belonged in Gryffindor, Hufflepuff, Ravenclaw or Slytherin will be excited to realize that, if they can pass Harvard University's competitive admissions process, they have a chance to belong to a house of their own. It speaks to the singularity of Harvard University as an institution that the houses are both needed and also put into effect. With a total of more than twenty thousand students and a rigorous and competitive academic program, houses break down the large student body into smaller, more manageable, support groups. Besides encouraging a sense of community, the houses also offer academic and personal support to Harvard University's students. As in the Harry Potter novels, a senior member of the faculty heads each house.

Today, there are twelve houses at Harvard University. Adams House, which celebrated its seventy-fifth anniversary in 2007, is the oldest of the twelve. Adams House doesn't consist of just one building. A number of buildings belong to the house, altogether making up something greater than its original parts. One of the residency halls for Adams House is Randolph Hall, built in 1897 by Archibald Cary Coolidge so his brother, a burgeoning architect, could have a quiet place to live on campus that was modeled after the dormitories at Oxford. The creation of Randolph Hall was the source of some historic strife.

Coolidge butted heads with one Charles Wetmore during the construction of Randolph Hall. Charles Wetmore was also in the process of building a dormitory on campus, a completely over-the-top luxury residence hall that would eventually feature private steam baths and an indoor swimming pool that has now, sadly, been filled in. Wetmore was concerned that when Randolph Hall was completed, it would block sunlight from reaching the rooms in his own building. Wetmore demanded that Coolidge set his building back by ten feet on the Linden Street side. Coolidge refused. In a fit of pique, Wetmore bought the property where the Harvard Lampoon building stands today and threatened to build a ten-story monstrosity that would keep the sun from ever touching the walls or windows of Randolph Hall.

Wetmore had won the fight. If you look at Randolph Hall today, you will see it is precisely ten feet from Linden Street. But Coolidge should get some respect for his dedication to Randolph Hall. The Boston native has been spied by students roaming the hallways of Randolph Hall since his death in 1928. He is often seen peering from the windows at the strip of grass that stands between the building and Linden Street. Whatever else you can say about Archibald Cary Coolidge, he doesn't let go of grudges very easily.

Dormitories are not the only haunted Harvard University buildings you'll find. The Harvard Lampoon building has some ghosts of its own. The building, which is also known as the Lampoon Castle, is said to be modeled after an old church that the designer, a Harvard alumni named Edmund Wheelwright, saw in Virginia. The building certainly is known for its unusual design. Seen head-on, it looks uncannily like a human face, complete with a spiked hat. It's a design not everyone loves. A former Cambridge mayor, Alfred Vellucci, once famously called it "one of the ugliest buildings in the world" located in an area that "is an ideal spot for a restroom." Vellucci would go on to propose an unsuccessful city ordinance declaring the Lampoon building a public urinal.

The spat between Vellucci and the Harvard Lampoon building was a funny one for anyone watching it from the outside, which should have endeared Vellucci at least a little bit to the staff at the *Lampoon*. After all, laughter is their business. The Harvard Lampoon building is the home to the *Harvard Lampoon*, which got its start back in 1876 when seven Harvard University undergrads got together and decided to create a publication modeled after the British humor magazine *Punch*. The first edition appeared in February, and the first print run of 1,200 sold out almost immediately.

In the early days of the magazine, jokes that came at the expense of Harvard University were a given, and no person, no matter how rich, famous or powerful, was exempt from being a target of the *Harvard Lampoon*. Also high on the list of farcical targets were popular magazines and the *Harvard Crimson*, which is the university's daily student paper. The *Harvard Lampoon* is still going strong today. It has dropped its sharply pointed pokes at Harvard University as it is now popular among a nationwide audience. Other than that, you'll still find it chock full of parodies, humorous cartoons and flat-out funny satires.

And even if the fine folks at the *Harvard Lampoon* didn't care for Vellucci's jabs at their beloved building, they may have gotten the last laugh. During his years as mayor, Vellucci planted a tree on city land to try and hide the face of the Lampoon Castle. The *Harvard Lampoon* countered the move by doing what it does best—publishing satirical pieces on Vellucci. Between the 1960s and 1980s, vandalism to the tree was common. It was even doused in acid twice. Finally, in 1991, in the cover of darkness, the tree was chopped down completely. The *Harvard Lampoon* refused to comment on the matter, neither confirming nor denying responsibility for the decimated tree. The city planted another, smaller tree. This one lasted only three years before, on the night of Harvard University's commencement, it, too, was chopped down. This time, the *Harvard Lampoon* stepped up to say it had not chopped down the tree. It did suggest, rather slyly, that the city should probably investigate whether the *Harvard Crimson* might be responsible.

Somehow, in between all these pranks, the *Harvard Lampoon* manages to produce the world's longest continually published humor magazine. Even dealing with the very active ghost that resides inside the Lampoon Castle can't seem to slow it down. Yes, that's right. Inside the grinning face of the Harvard Lampoon building is a restless spirit that roams the many halls and passageways of the building. Just how many rooms are there in there? You might be surprised to find out. There are even some secret passages inside—but just how many and where they might lead on campus is a closely held secret.

The ghost would be a good person to ask. The male figure, wearing an old 1900s suit, knows the building better than anyone. He's been there nearly since construction was complete on the building. Former *Lampoon* staffers say he is the perfect addition to the building, not too hardworking and always up for shenanigans. Someone should consider his part in those missing city trees.

LESLEY UNIVERSITY

CAMBRIDGE

Online, in newspaper articles and in books, you can find lots of mentions of ghosts at Lesley University. The only problem is that actual details about the university's hauntings are very hard to come by. Finding a student who will own up to experiencing a ghost on campus is even harder. But there's a good reason why Lesley University's Avon Hill buildings might feature a ghost or two and why they might just be so terrifying that no one wants to talk about them.

Today, Cambridge's Avon Hill neighborhood sits in a desirable location, wedged between Harvard and Porter Squares. The addition of the Lesley University campus has added new life and color to this already vibrant area of Cambridge. But in the early days of the city of Cambridge, it sat on the outskirts of town and wasn't really sought after by much of anyone. Because of a small hill of just about eighty feet that sat in this unused portion on the edge of the city that made it very visible to the surrounding area, it became the site of the city's gallows.

Of course, the area instantly became known around Massachusetts as Gallows Hill. There's no telling how many people met death on Gallows Hill during the nearly two hundred years it was put to that purpose. The most famous case to ever come to an end on Gallows Hill happened in 1755.

Two slaves, named Mark and Phillis, were found guilty of killing their master, a man named Captain John Codman. The murder was done using poison because Mark, who could read, had scoured the Bible looking for a way to complete the crime without inducing sin on himself or his co-

conspirators. He had concluded that poison didn't count as murder because no blood was shed. This belief might have been helped along by a long-standing rumor among Cambridge's slave population that a Mr. Salmon, a notoriously cruel slave owner, had been poisoned to death by a slave without the crime ever being discovered by the authorities.

Mark and Phillis did not get off as easily as Mr. Salmon's killer. They were quickly found guilty and sentenced to death. Mark was hanged on Gallows Hill before his body was moved to Charlestown to be left to decompose chained to a pole as a warning to any other slaves who might think of rebelling against their masters. Mark's body would remain gibbeted in this way in Charlestown for twenty years and would become a grisly landmark of sorts. Paul Revere would even make note of Mark's body in a letter he later wrote about his infamous midnight ride.

"After I had passed Charlestown Neck, and got nearly opposite where Mark was hung in chains, I saw two men on horseback under a tree," Revere wrote in the letter.

It was an unusual punishment for the crime. Gibbeting was, as a general rule, a punishment more often used for pirates. Phillis, too, met an unlikely end for his part in the death of Captain John Codman. Phillis was burned at the stake, one of only two people to meet this fate in Massachusetts history. The other was also an African slave, this one a young woman who was convicted of attempting to murder her master when she set his house on fire.

In 1817, the courthouse and jail were moved to a different Cambridge location. Within a few years, the fine people of Cambridge found themselves using Gallows Hill less and less often now that it was not so conveniently located next to where the prisoners were being kept and tried. By the mid-1800s, Gallows Hill was completely abandoned and finally sold by the city. In time, even the name Gallows Hill would fall into disuse and later be replaced by the far more politically correct name Avon Hill, which borrowed its name from nearby Avon Street.

This small sub-neighborhood of Cambridge is a hotbed of paranormal activity, though few residents today seem to know that the cause is most likely due to the extreme number of deaths that once occurred here. Highly emotional events such as murders, suicides and, yes, executions seem to have sparked unexplainable phenomena that continue for years to come even as the original sources of the haunting disappear into the fogs of time.

MOUNT HOLYOKE COLLEGE

SOUTH HADLEY

If real-life ghost stories and urban legends weren't popular among Massachusetts's colleges and universities, there wouldn't be so many of them and this book wouldn't exist. But even considering the enormous prevalence of these kinds of stories in general, Mount Holyoke College's student body still wins the title of "Most Ghost Crazy" out of all the schools in this book.

There are several student-run blogs and websites dedicated to collecting the paranormal experiences students have had on the Mount Holyoke campus. The fact that they all mostly cover the same ground and all of them make it a point to debunk the most popular myths on campus has done nothing to slow down their proliferation. College finder websites and chat rooms are full of threads where Mount Holyoke College students debate which dorm is best to move into—taking ghosts into consideration, of course.

The college certainly has a lot to take pride in when it comes to ghosts. Find any article or book on haunted colleges in America and you'll usually find Mount Holyoke College featured prominently in it. In 2004, a film crew from Authentic Entertainment spent several days on the Mount Holyoke College campus taping a segment on haunted colleges for the Travel Channel.

Still, despite the sheer plentitude of ghost stories around Mount Holyoke College, it's hard to tell exactly why there's so much interest from the student body in the college's hauntings. Lots of schools are just as haunted as Mount Holyoke seems to be, and there's barely any interest from the student body at all. It may be simply because of the attitude of the school administration itself.

Unlike some schools that try to hide their ghosts, Mount Holyoke College tends to take a different approach. Haunted tours of the school are fairly common around Halloween, and various other ghost-related activities around school seem to be encouraged as lovely traditions that add to the full college experience rather than being seen as silly distractions that should be squashed.

One of these traditions is the peculiar, although not particularly ghostly, practice of eating ice cream in freezing cold early morning hours in November at the grave of the school's founder, Mary Lyon. Luckily, the start of this odd tradition has not been obscured by time, and it's interesting to see the evolution of the now annual ceremony.

The tradition began as a snipe hunt of sorts that upperclassmen sent the incoming freshman on. In 1910, someone had the idea to tell a group of these fresh-faced young freshmen that if they showed up at Mary Lyon's grave at 6:00 a.m. on Founders Day, which was traditionally held the Sunday nearest to November 8, they would find the school's trustees churning ice cream. And for whatever reason, some of these freshman decided that getting up in the early morning hours on a day they had no classes to stand in the freezing cold and watch their school trustees making ice cream was a fine idea.

The upperclassmen who started the rumor thought seeing the poor, shivering freshman standing alongside the wrought-iron fence around the grave was so funny that they kept the joke going. Each year, there would be a new crop of naïve freshmen, and each year, honestly, the joke seemed a little less funny. Eventually, in 1920, a small group of seniors took pity on the poor, gullible freshman and met them in the cold at Mary Lyon's grave with ice cream cones in hand.

Once word got around that there really was ice cream to be had at Mary Lyon's grave on Founder's Day morning, the whole thing snowballed. Eventually, school officials did take over the ice cream scooping, and minus a few years during World War II when everyone was tightening their belts thanks to war rationing, the tradition has gone on unabated. Unabated, that is, with one minor difference. Now that there really is ice cream, freshmen are no longer welcome. This is, as an unspoken sort of law, a seniors-only event.

If the ice cream eating at the founder's grave tradition seems a little strange, here's another peculiar part about the whole thing. The place where everyone meets on Founder's Day, Mary Lyon's grave—there's a chance that there's no body buried there at all. There has been some debate, pretty much since Mary Lyon died in 1849, on exactly where it is that she ended up being buried.

Mount Holyoke College maintains, as you would expect the school to, that Mary Lyon is most definitely buried beneath the tombstone where generations of Mount Holyoke students have consumed countless gallons of ice cream over the years. But other sources, contemporary to her death, say she was actually interred in a family cemetery in her hometown of Buckland, Massachusetts.

Just to add another layer of improbability to everything surrounding Mary Lyon's grave, there is a third unlikely story about her burial. In this story, the revered founder dies, is publically laid out in the seminary building on the Mount Holyoke campus and then, before the funeral can commence, a group of students from Wheaton College, of which Mary Lyon was also a founder, steal the body and bring it back to their school to bury it.

In yet another version of this (hopefully) tall tale, trustees at Mount Holyoke College catch the Wheaton body snatchers in the act and quickly bury Mary Lyon themselves on Mount Holyoke College grounds. The crew from Wheaton is so incensed by this that they come back that very night, dig her up and move her body in secret to Wheaton College.

With so many stories rising around Mary Lyon, it should come as no surprise that she is the subject of a ghost story or two on campus as well. The origins of the ghostly legend seem about as likely as the story of her body being robbed from its grave by loyal Wheaton students. But that doesn't mean that Mary Lyon and her associates don't still wander the campus she helped create back in 1837.

The most popular legend about Mary Lyon centers on an illicit love affair. In the early days, back when Mary Lyon first created the Mount Holyoke Female Seminary, the story says she fell madly in love with Deacon Porter, a staunch supporter of the school. Porter felt as strongly about Mary as she felt for him, but there was one very big problem: Deacon Porter was already married. Eventually, Porter's wife, Hannah, discovered the affair between her husband and Mary Lyon. As you can imagine, Hannah Porter was not pleased. After a near knock-'em-down brawl, Hannah swore revenge on Mary Lyon.

In life, the best Hannah Porter could do was to keep the two lovers apart. But she was a woman scorned, and that simply wasn't good enough for her. So after her death, Hannah began haunting her own portrait, hung in a Mount Holyoke College dormitory. Hannah's hatred for Mary Lyon extended even to the students at the college that Mary founded and loved so much. Female students who had the misfortune of resembling Mary Lyon found themselves plagued by unexplained incidents. Schoolwork went missing, the doors to their rooms wouldn't stay locked and everywhere they went in the dormitory they felt watched by the hateful eyes of Hannah Porter's portrait.

There is no contemporary evidence to back up anything from this persistent legend. There is no proof outside the oft-repeated story itself that Mary Lyon and Deacon Porter were ever anything more or less than professional colleagues. All records dating from the time around the founding of the college point to Mary Lyon being an extremely serious and religious woman who, it seems, would be unlikely to have had a love affair at all—and certainly not with a married man. Besides such an act being against the rules of her church, it also would have been illegal under Massachusetts's adultery laws at the time. It seems more than a little farfetched that Mary Lyon would have risked her reputation, her freedom and the future of the school to which she was so dedicated for the part-time love of a married man.

Of course, not all of Mount Holyoke College's ghosts have some connection to the school's founder, Mary Lyon. Like many colleges and universities, Mount Holyoke has a ghost said to be the result of a former student's suicide. The girl is said to have thrown herself from the roof of South Mandelle, a Mount Holyoke College residence hall. If it were possible to judge a building's hauntedness by how it looks, the twin dormitories, North and South Mandelle, could probably win joint awards for creepiest place on earth.

Looking like something out of a gothic novel, the buildings are four stories tall, built of weathered reddish brick and feature an overwhelming assortment of gables, turrets, chimneys and tower rooms. They have a forgotten, ancient and haunting air on a bright sunny day. Late at night or during one of Massachusetts's overcast gray fall days, they are downright uncanny.

The ghost of the suicide keeps her former dorm room locked, much to the chagrin of any student assigned to stay there who forgets to keep her keys on her at all times. In the 1970s, a student named Jane was said to be so plagued by this spirit that it followed her even after she fled the haunted room. Eventually, Jane left Mount Holyoke College altogether.

Not to be outdone by its sister, North Mandelle has a creepy ghost that lacks the suicide backstory. While no one is sure who this spirit is, she has been seen many times over the years by students, staff and visitors to the school.

April wasn't a resident in North Mandelle, and being new to Mount Holyoke College, she had not yet heard the ghost stories about this particular residence hall. One time, after a long night's studying session, a friend offered to let April sleep in her North Mandelle room while she went out to find the girls something to eat.

April curled up in the bed in the smaller of the two rooms in the second-floor suite. She fell asleep almost immediately. Sometime later, she was awakened by the strange feeling of being watched. She figured her friend had returned to the room with a pizza. But as she sat up, still half asleep in the bed, she saw a strange woman with wild eyes staring at her from the corner.

The woman said nothing—she barely even moved—and April decided she must still be asleep. She murmured a half-garbled "Go away," pulled the blanket over her head and rolled over. A little while later, her friend did return. When April began to tell her about the strange dream, the friend nearly screamed.

"You saw the lady in the corner," the friend gasped, cutting April off before she could get too far into her tale.

The friend said that she, too, had been awakened nearly every night by the image of the wild-eyed woman for the first few weeks she was in the suite. As April had already experienced for herself, the woman never said anything and never moved from the corner. Eventually, the girl had worked up her nerve one night to tell the spirit to leave her alone. She never saw her again after that and eventually decided it had been her mind playing tricks on her. The two girls started quietly asking around and eventually found several students who had all seen the same woman, or knew of someone who had seen the woman, in the same room.

Wilder Hall, another of Mount Holyoke College's dormitories, is also said to be plagued by the spirit of a suicide. This ghost story goes two steps further in that it claims that every student who ever lived in the room where the suicide occurred went on to later break her legs in freak accidents and that the school eventually got so tired of seeing students limping around campus in casts and crutches that they closed off the room despite a housing crunch.

While Mount Holyoke College's archives don't record a spate of suicides or broken limbs, there is no denying that the stairwell next to this locked room has a reputation for being seriously bad news. Students avoid the stairwell thanks to its roving cold spots, the general creepy feeling within and, some claim, because students are known for tripping over nothing while trying to traverse the stairs.

On one Mount Holyoke College ghost website, a student named Christina recounts the story of her experience living next to this haunted stairwell. Christina says that while her room was fine, she, too, avoided the stairs at all costs. One night, a friend from out of state came to visit her and was intrigued by the ghost story. The friend, a girl named Penny, convinced Christina to give her a tour of the stairwell and the sealed-off room.

The stairs were cold, as usual, but uneventful. Penny grew frustrated with the lack of ghostly activity. Outside the door to the sealed room, she started taunting the ghosts, asking them to give her a sign if they were real.

To the surprise of both girls, a loud banging started up from inside the locked, empty room. It sounded exactly as if someone on the other side was forcefully thumping the door with her fist. Christina had been living on the fourth floor of Wilder Hall for some time and had never heard noises like this before from anywhere in the building—never mind from a room that everyone on campus knew was locked and empty!

Shortly after this event, there was a windstorm that tore through South Hadley, tearing down trees and causing lots of damage. One of these downed trees crashed into Wilder Hall, smashing through the roof above the locked dorm room. Since that time, there has been no more reported ghostly activity from the room, or the stairwell next to it, and students speculate that the destruction somehow released the unhappy spirit from the room where she had died.

Torrey Hall is somewhat unique when it comes to Mount Holyoke College's residence buildings. Built in 1949, it has a more modern air than dorm buildings like Mandelle or Wilder Hall. That doesn't mean that it's any less haunted, though.

Athletes tend to prefer living at Torrey Hall due to its proximity to the Kendall Sports and Dance Complex. Another bonus to living at Torrey Hall that isn't talked much about by school administrators is that there is a ghostly housekeeper on board the staff. The sound of a broom being slowly swept up and down the corridors, and the faint but unmistakable sound of someone humming as they push it along, has been reported by students almost since the creation of the building.

There may be a second spirit in the building, though this one is not nearly as useful as the unseen housekeeper. A few students have been awakened by the booming sound of a man's laughter in their rooms. So far, no one has seen either ghost or come up with a good backstory as to how they got there.

Buckland Hall is considered to be the sister structure to Torrey Hall. Both were built around the same time by Douglas Orr, and they share a certain resemblance to each other for this reason. Buckland Hall also has a ghost in residence, which, like those in Torrey Hall, is heard and sensed but has never been seen, at least not yet.

This spirit makes itself known with the prerequisite cold spots and creepy-crawly feelings. But its invisible presence also makes an impression in other ways—namely, in the furniture. Upon feeling that there is a force sharing space with them, students say they hear a man's heavy footsteps walk around the room until eventually they see the shape of an invisible body settle onto the edge of a bed or in a favorite reading chair. Some students have gone so far as to add extra seating to their rooms to try and keep the ghost from climbing into bed with them.

Porter Hall, the very first new dormitory to be built on campus after a fire ripped through the Mount Holyoke Seminary building, is home to a classic lady in white–style haunting. Lady in white hauntings are something of a universal ghostly archetype, and many cultures across many time periods have reported this kind of spirit. Despite the many ladies in white and the various mythologies of the people and places that report them, the stories are always surprisingly similar. As the name implies, this kind of ghost is seen as a white-clad woman; some stories go so far as to describe her as wearing a wedding dress. Her story is usually one of lost love or betrayal by her fiancé or newlywed husband. In England and Scotland, ladies in white are often considered to be more like banshees than regular ghosts. They are tied to a particular family, and if anyone in the family sees the ghost, it is taken as a sign that he or she will be the next to die. In the United States, ladies in white are almost never seen in this way. Instead, they are tied to a place, usually one where they took their own life or had their life taken by the one they loved and trusted the most.

While the legends about the Porter Hall ghost vary depending on who is doing the telling, they always seem to fall into the typical range for these

kinds of hauntings. She was betrayed by a lover or kept from marrying a beloved fiancé and now roams the building in a white wedding gown.

The interesting thing about Porter Hall's lady is that she seems to have formed an attachment to various students over the years. Many a student has been awakened from sound slumber to see the glowing white form floating directly above her roommate's head—or, even worse, her own!

The ghost seems to stick with these students. She isn't tied to a particular room or place unless it's the building as a whole. So far, no common thread has been found that links all these students together. Most begin their relationship with the lady in white thoroughly freaked out. Quickly, they find that, as far as ghosts go, their new BFF is pretty easy to deal with.

NORTHERN ESSEX COMMUNITY COLLEGE

HAVERHILL

Northern Essex Community College is a unique addition to this collection of haunted schools for three reasons. First, it's one of the few community colleges to make the grade as far as ghost stories are concerned. Second, it's not haunted in the slightest, at least as far as anyone has come forward to say. And third, it is the only college in this book that offers a class in ghost hunting.

This class, "Paranormal CSI: Ghost Hunting 101," is a new addition to Northern Essex Community College's non-credit personal enrichment offerings. It began being offered to students in the spring of 2012. The instructor for the class is Ronald Kolek, executive director of the New England Ghost Project.

While Kolek's ghost-hunting group contains the usual assortment of mediums and sensitives who tend to gravitate to these kinds of endeavors, much of the class offered at Northern Essex Community focuses on the more scientific side of ghost hunting. Over the course of six weeks, students learn the how's and why's of using everything from cameras to audio recordings. Besides this crash course in ghost-hunting equipment, students also get the chance to test out their skills against some actual ghosts.

Because of the college's uncommonly non-haunted condition, students in "Paranormal CSI: Ghost Hunting 101" had to go off campus to put their newly acquired knowledge into practice. Kolek brought students on a field trip of sorts to the Veasey Estate in Groveland, Massachusetts. It's a site that Kolek had visited, along with the New England Ghost Project, several times in the past and is supposed to be heavily haunted.

Northern Essex Community College hasn't let the fact that it isn't haunted keep it from offering ghost-hunting courses for its students. *Photo courtesy of Jeff Titus.*

The estate sits in the center of Veasey Memorial Park. Originally, the home and park were the fifty-acre summer estate of mill owner Arthur D. Veasey. During their most profitable years, Veasey's mills made textiles that would go on to be used in the manufacture of the seats of cars on Ford's assembly line. But by the time the Great Depression rolled around, the mills were dismantled, and Veasey was forced to sell his summer estate in Groveland. The property went rapidly through a series of owners until, in the 1950s, it was bought by the Little Missionary Sisters of Charity.

The nuns turned the property into something that was part hospital, part halfway house for adult women with a variety of special needs. Many of these women were placed here by families that were all too happy to hide their afflictions from the prying eyes of the world. Others were former mental patients at Danvers State Mental Institution—a very haunted site in its own right until recent years, when it was torn down and turned into high-priced condos.

In 1996, the Town of Groveland bought the property and turned it into a memorial park. Since then, many have found the nine-thousand-square-foot Veasey house to be filled with haunts. There is an older woman and a young girl who are often seen together hovering around the kitchen of the home. Various other specters have been seen or felt as cold spots throughout the former home.

Dorna Caskie, an events manager at Veasey Memorial Park, had a far less tangible but still intriguing experience one night at the Veasey Estate. She told Boston.com's Taryn Plumb that she spent one night in the house with her two children. All three were awakened at 3:00 a.m. by nothing they could name. All three later described feeling a very intense electric feeling for no good reason at all.

"I felt like I was in a room full of very excited and very happy children," Caskie told the reporter.

Mediums who accompanied Ronald Kolek to the site in the past have described feeling spirits from the 1940s in the home's living room and a male energy that haunts the basement. While they were unable to explain the woman and girl in the kitchen, both psychics sensed something to do with head trauma.

Certainly, with that many ghosts running around, students of the "Paranormal CSI: Ghost Hunting 101" class had lots of opportunities to put their newfound knowledge to use. Perhaps with so many new ghost hunters among the ranks of the enrolled, someone will soon dig up a haunting or two on the Northern Essex Community College campus itself.

PINE MANOR COLLEGE

CHESTNUT HILL

A nn was just approaching the Main House at Pine Manor College when she started to get the terrible feeling that she was being watched. She stopped in her tracks, turning around slowly while scanning the area around her, but could find no evidence of anyone being in the nearby vicinity. Up ahead, the lights in the Main House were shining brightly, and she started

walking a little more quickly toward them, unable to shake the feeling that she was being followed.

As Ann came across the building, the formerly comforting lights started to blink out one by one. She was plunged into total darkness. The overwhelming feeling of danger washed over her. She didn't stop to think. She just started to run.

As soon as she was past the building, she turned again, sure that she had heard heavy footsteps in fast pursuit. Again, no one was there. But each and every light that had winked out as she had run past the Main House was once again shining brightly. Ann would never forget the strange thing that happened that night, though in time she began to think that she must have imagined the entire thing.

If Ann had asked around campus, she probably could have found more than a few other students who shared similar stories. What the force is at Pine Manor College is unknown, but students have reported these kinds of stories for years. Others have been so unnerved by the presence that they've ducked into the nearby woods to hide from whomever it was they felt was following them. But the woods offer little sanctuary. Many say they found themselves encircled by a dense freezing cold mist even on warm summer nights.

Regis College

WESTON

Until recently, Regis College was a private four-year Roman Catholic women's college in Weston, Massachusetts. It wasn't until 2007 that the school started opening its admissions to men, making it the last Catholic women's college in the Boston area to become coeducational. The school was started in 1927 by the Sisters of St. Joseph of Boston, and its campus now encompasses 132 acres in Weston, Massachusetts, just miles from downtown Boston. Regis College is consistently ranked, by both the *U.S. News and World Report* and the *Princeton Review*, as one of the best colleges in the Northeast. It's also a great college for ghost hunters.

College Hall, built in the late 1920s, has several ghosts spread across several floors of the oversized five-story building. On the second floor of College Hall, located within its grand foyer, there are reports of the ghost of a former piano teacher. While this ghost most often announces its presence by opening and shutting doors until politely asked to stop, a few students have reported actually seeing the spirit. Many

College Hall, the first structure built by Regis College after purchasing the Morrison Estate, has several ghosts in residence.

students have been unnerved enough by this seemingly innocuous spirit to get campus security involved. The security guards hate to spread the ghost stories associated with the college, but most will admit to having experienced the door-slamming ghost themselves. Several even admit to having heard ghostly strains of beautiful piano music drifting up around the foyer, played by an unseen hand in the middle of the night.

If you're looking to see a ghost, and not just hear one, the fourth floor of College Hall is a better bet than the grand foyer. Here you'll find the spirits of several nuns, thought to be founding members of the staff at Regis College, wearing their full habits as they wander the hallways. They are usually preceded by the sound of rosary beads clanking together as they walk. The nuns are seen as a benign presence. When they've encountered the living, they are said to give a gentle nod and to continue on their nightly walks as if they have no idea that they are no longer among the living themselves.

Unfortunately, there is also a less benevolent presence in College Hall. Many students find themselves inexplicably overcome with feelings of dread and hopelessness when they're in the building's elevator or stairwell. The feelings of despair go hand in hand with walking into an overwhelming cold spot that many say roams the building. These sudden drops in ambient temperature are thought by paranormal researchers to be significant evidence of a ghostly presence. Ghost hunters believe these cold spots are all that remain of a weak spirit, one that lacks enough energy to manifest itself in any other way. Cold spots can seem to latch onto the living, and it is believed that this is the spirit trying to draw enough energy to make itself seen. While cold spots are usually not dangerous, the one floating around College Hall creates such a strong emotional reaction in the living that it should be avoided as much as possible. Local rumor holds that it is all that remains of the spirit of a former student or staff member who committed suicide in the building shortly after it was built.

There are some reports of other ghosts on campus, although most of the well-known activity takes place in College Hall. Walters Hall and the radio station located in Alumnae Hall have had spatterings of ghost stories associated with them over the years.

SALEM STATE UNIVERSITY

SALEM

I t really should come as no surprise to anyone that Salem State University, the only college or university to be found in Salem, Massachusetts, would make it into a book on haunted schools. You would expect nothing less from a city famous for being the site of the very real House of Seven Gables, a city that is home to one of the largest and most open pagan populations in the world and one that is famous for something as spectacularly spooky as the Salem Witch Trials.

Of course, a town that celebrates Halloween all October long and that once hanged nineteen people and pressed another one to death under heavy stones because of wild tales of witches and demons *would* have a haunted college in its midst. Sadly, many will find the ghost stories that come from Salem State University to not quite live up to Salem's witchy reputation. While the tourism board would probably love to be able to promote stories of a demon or two wandering the hallways, or maybe an accused witch dripping pools of ghostly water as she relives her water torture, the ghosts at Salem State University have much more modern roots.

Like many other universities, Salem State's most well-known spirit can be found in one of the school's dormitories. Room 222 of first-year residence building Bowditch Hall may just be the most haunted place on campus.

The true story behind this haunting has been obscured thanks to a persistent and entirely fictitious story about three students being murdered in the room in the 1970s. As is often the case with these kinds of campus urban legends about murders and suicide, it appears to have no basis in fact whatsoever. But that certainly hasn't stopped the story from being handed down again and again to each new generation of Salem State University students.

While it's easy for those on the outside to laugh off these kinds of obviously exaggerated and made-up tales, students who are assigned to the room find them to be no laughing matter. They realize pretty quickly that even if the story about how the ghost got there was made up, the ghost itself seems to be very, very real.

The first sign that students in room 222 get that things are about to become strange during their first year in college is the loud banging inside the walls of the room. The noise can only be heard inside the room itself—but once you're inside, what a noise it is! These are not the clanks and groans of pipes expanding within the walls. These are an all-out wake-you-up-in-the-middle-of-the-night, make-you-jump-straight-out-of-bed alarm coming directly from the other side. How they can't be heard from the hallways outside the room is an utter mystery.

And on those nights when you don't get woken up by a frantic banging in the walls, you can look forward to the equally alarming shaking of the bed. And no, these aren't gentle little rocking movements that softly bring you to wakefulness from your carefree slumber. Students who have experienced it themselves say they have literally been shaken right out of bed and onto the floor.

The students who have had run-ins with this spirit seem evenly split as to what they think its intent might be. Some see it as a purely malignant force. And it's easy to see where they would get that impression. Try explaining to the professor of your morning class that you overslept because a ghost was banging on your walls all night before knocking you out of bed.

Others feel the sense that the ghost did meet some kind of ill fate in the room, even if it's not the three disco-loving spirits of murder victims, and that the entity's distraught alarms are meant to protect the student from meeting a similar fate. The constant need to wake students up from their much-needed sleep is sure to drive residents to their wits' end, but maybe it's a little easier to swallow if they think the ghost really does have their best interests at heart. Without knowing the true backstory behind this haunting, it makes it nearly impossible to know the ghost's true intent.

Whatever the objective of the ghost in Bowditch Hall, there is another spot on campus that definitely does have a protective spirit watching over students and staff alike. Salem State University's Mainstage Auditorium is just as haunted as any good theater should be.

At first glance, the story behind this ghost seems nearly as unbelievable as the one about three murder victims in Bowditch Hall. The legend is that a small child, or in some versions a drunken teenager, named Tommy was fooling around in a crawl space above the theater one night and fell to his death. The body was discovered the next day by a professor who was taking part in an upcoming theater performance. The story certainly sounds like the typical urban legend with little concrete evidence to back it up.

The area where Tommy is said to have fallen has been mostly boarded up in the forty or so years that have passed since this terrible accident is supposed to have happened. The little bit of the space that is still accessible is used mostly for long-term storage. You would never guess that, though, from the noises that emanate from this space—fast-running footsteps, murmurs of laughter and singing, unexplained crashes. Really, it's hard to believe that there's only one spirit and not an entire small army of ghosts tromping around up there. Or at least a lot of very active squirrels.

Before you go passing off the strange noises as simply a matter of random theater acoustics or rogue rodents, there is a lot more activity going on in the Mainstage Auditorium to back up the ghost story. Those who have had reason to climb up into the long-term storage space report feeling a hand pressing against their backs, as if something unseen were trying to keep them from falling. The overwhelming feeling of concern precedes this spirit, whoever he is, wherever he goes.

Smith College

Northampton

With alumnae ranging from Sylvia Plath to Nancy Reagan and from Julia Child to Betty Friedan, and the school's standing as the largest member of the Seven Sisters, Smith College really needs no introduction. The school itself dates from the late 1800s, but many of the buildings you'll find on the campus are much older structures. Unlike many colleges, Smith embraces its ghost stories wholeheartedly. They are seen as a colorful addition to campus folklore and history. The stories told on and about the Smith College campus run the gamut of darkly tragic and romantic to obvious old-fashioned moral tales whose popularity is most likely linked to the fact that the college has always been an all-girls' school.

One of these legends that walks the line between ghost story and morality lesson is about the spirit of Chase House. Chase House, one of the buildings on lower Elm Street, became a dorm building fairly recently, at least as far as Smith College history goes. Prior to the school purchasing the property in 1968, it had been the site of a girls' school dating back to the early 1870s. Before that, the building served as a boardinghouse for single workingwomen. One of the long-ago residents of this boardinghouse, a young girl who worked long hours in a factory, became pregnant out of wedlock. This is a scary enough situation for young women today, never mind the shame and scorn she would have faced as an unmarried mother 150 years ago.

The girl didn't know what to do. She tearfully confessed her condition to her best friend and fellow boarder. Together, they made a terrible pact. The

girl would conceal her pregnancy, her friend would help her deliver the baby in secret and then the two would do away with the child.

The child was delivered, somehow in secret, at the boardinghouse, and the two did go through with their plan to kill the baby. Shortly afterward, the mother fell ill from complications from her unaccompanied birth and died. Since then, as an article in the Smith College newspaper, *The Sophian*, put it, "she was reunited with her baby and now she carries it in her arms as she traverses the house. Her footsteps are clearly heard, and so are the occasional wails of the baby."

Talbot House is the scene of an equally tragic though much different kind of haunting. Built in 1909, the building was originally used as a private school for youngsters run by a Miss Bessie Capen. During its time as the Capen School, a little boy named Thomas was a student there. Thomas didn't quite fit in with the other kids and spent long hours playing by himself. One day, he was surprised when several of the older boys invited him to play hide-and-seek with them. But the invitation to play was just a ruse. The older boys convinced Thomas to climb up into an attic room, promising that they'd be right behind him. Instead, they slammed the ladder up and locked the door, leaving the young boy up there on his own. Teachers at the school noticed Thomas's absence fairly quickly, but it was still several days before anyone thought to look in the building's attic, a spot that was off limits to the students. By the time anyone did climb up to look, Thomas was the victim of hunger and dehydration.

A fourth-floor bathroom has since become a favorite place for Thomas. He flips the faucets on and off at will and flushes toilets one after another until an irritated student tells him to stop. One Family Weekend, a visiting mother ran into Thomas in the bathroom. The woman had a long conversation with him. As she walked out of the bathroom, she realized she hadn't said goodbye to the boy. When she turned to do so, she discovered he wasn't there.

Interestingly, Thomas stopped being seen and felt in the fourth-floor bathroom when Smith College began locking the door to the attic where he died. Thomas seems to not have realized that ghosts can easily pass through locked doors. Even so, students still report hearing his presence up in the building's attic. Fourth-floor residents sometimes hear a child's footsteps running around the attic and even faint knocking sounds on the locked attic door.

Talbot House is home to a second spirit. This one is, in many ways, a classic lady in white kind of specter. On the surface, the lady in white of Talbot House is one of these very typical sorts of ghosts. Most students who see her agree that she's wearing a wedding dress; others say it is a very ornate nightgown that looks like bridal wear to our more modern sensibilities. This lady in white runs across the porch of Talbot House, jumps over the railing and disappears into the ether on the other side just as if she was never there.

The one thing that separates Talbot House's ghost from the rest of her lady in white cousins is that there's no story to go along with her. She's not chasing down a fiancé who ultimately drags her into the woods and strangles her for her inheritance. She isn't running across the porch in a fright because her husband has tried to kill her. Instead, she's a mystery, one that many students claim to see but none pretends to understand.

Northrop House would be the perfect situation for a lady in white haunting, but this building's ghost takes a much different approach. The stories say that during one summer abroad, a Smith junior named Francine fell in love with a dashing Italian man. Their summer together was brief, but the couple made promises that they would stay true to each other and keep in constant contact even after Francine went home.

And that is precisely what happened when Francine first returned to her dorm at Northrop House—at least for the first few months. The two sent love letters constantly, and Francine excitedly told her classmates that they had made plans to elope as soon as she was done with school. But as time went on, the letters from Francine's Italian lover got shorter and shorter and started coming more and more sporadically. Eventually, Francine was sending tear-stained letters and getting nothing in return.

The poor girl was heartbroken. She didn't know if she had done something wrong or if her lover had gotten injured and couldn't contact her or if he had simply just changed his mind about her and didn't have the courage to say so. Midway into her senior year, Francine left Smith College, leaving her possessions behind, and was not seen or heard from again.

Or at least she was not heard from again in life.

A rocking chair that had been left behind in Francine's haste to leave Smith College quickly got a reputation for having a mind of its own. Students who sat in the chair got chills. Sometimes the chair would gaily rock back and forth all on its own, stopping only when someone demanded that Francine stop playing around. Word got around that the chair was creepy, and eventually someone had the sense to do away with the piece of furniture altogether.

Things remained quiet in Northrop House until 1968. That year, out of sheer dumb luck, a student moved into Francine's old room and just happened to bring a rocking chair with her. This new piece of furniture quickly developed the same problems that had plagued Francine's rocking chair years earlier.

Attics at Smith College seem to be attractive to ghosts. Besides the spirit of Thomas over in Talbot House, there are two other campus buildings that have very active upper stories. Baldwin House has a great deal of activity in its uppermost floor during the night hours. The usual ghostly footsteps are, of course, a common report. Students are assured that no one is up there because the attic door is always kept locked. But more disturbing are the sounds that students describe as someone dragging something very heavy and wet back and forth across the floor all night long.

Interestingly, there are less common, but very intriguing, reports of students finding damp footprints leading from one section of the fourth floor up to the attic. A look into the history of the building shows that these footprints start at a spot that was once a bathroom, long ago renovated away by Smith College to a new purpose. It is unclear how the damp footprints and the dragging in the attic might be connected, but it seems likely that they must be.

The building at 150 Elm Street has plenty of knocking going on in its attic as well. For some students, it's a nightly occurrence. As soon as they turn off their lights and get ready to sleep, knocking begins in their ceiling and the walls directly above their headboards. Other students in the same room claim to hear nothing at all.

Park House has the rare ghost story that can be tied to a definite student and a definitive event. The Smith archives confirm that on November 13, 1925, a freak accident took the life of one of the school's students. Jeanne M. Robeson was a Smith College senior living in Park House when she became the victim of a series of small events that ultimately led to her death. Robeson was in the kitchen at Park House ironing her laundry when she, for whatever reason, decided to turn on the gas stove. Before she could light the stove, she tripped over something, or perhaps fainted, and hit her head on the way down, knocking herself unconscious. Breathing in the fumes from the stove, Robeson didn't have a chance. What would probably have only been a minor blackout turned into full-blown unconsciousness. Robeson had closed the kitchen door, probably so as not to wake her classmates, who were sleeping in rooms off the hallway where the kitchen was located. Everyone else living in the building was none the wiser as to what had befallen the girl. By the time morning rolled around, she had asphyxiated.

Since that time, Robeson has been a busy presence in Park House. Most students find her a reassuring force. She has a strong, and understandable, concern for the well-being of Park House's residents, and many of those girls say that Robeson has stopped them from falling or forgetting their work or saved them from countless other incidents big and small.

The only downside to Robeson's presence is that she's a little unclear on how to operate the technology of today—or maybe she fears it might bring some harm to the students she works so hard to watch over. Cellphones go wild when Jeanne Robeson is around, MP3 players refuse to work at all and students with Kindles, Nooks or tablets beware. They're found moved all over dorm rooms, tipped upside down or tucked in with papers and trash. Jeanne can't seem to make heads or tails of what they are actually supposed to do. One can only imagine what will happen when the day comes that she figures out how to turn them on.

The oldest building on the Smith College campus, and in fact one of the oldest buildings still standing in the town of Northampton, is Sessions House. Not surprisingly, it's also the scene of the school's most well-known ghost story. The home was built in 1751 by Captain John Hunt. At the time it was built, the home was very much on the outskirts of town and more or less cut off from neighbors. Hunt had the home built with a secret room under the main stairwell so his family could hide if the local Native American population ever turned against them and attacked. The room saw no real use until many years later, during the Revolutionary War, when it was put to a much different purpose.

General John "Gentleman Johnnie" Burgoyne, a general of the British army, was injured in battle and then captured by the Revolutionary forces near Northampton in 1777. During his imprisonment and recovery period, he was kept at the home of Captain Jonathan Hunt. Gentleman Johnnie didn't have much to do while staying in the Hunt home; luckily for him, Jonathan Hunt had several daughters. One of these girls was roughly Gentleman Johnnie's age, and as can probably be expected, she quickly fell for the dashing young military man.

Of course, it was a relationship that couldn't be. But like many young lovers forbidden to see each other, Lucy Hunt and Johnnie Burgoyne couldn't keep away from each other. They made the secret room under the stairs their nightly meeting spot for the several months he stayed at the house. Somehow the two avoided being caught by Lucy's parents, and by the time Gentleman Johnnie was better and sent back home to England, they had decided they were in love.

Johnnie swore he'd find a way to return to Lucy. But fate was not on the young lover's side. Johnnie was sent back to England and then rapidly sent back out to fight in Ireland. He'd never make his way back to the United States. Lucy, for her part, did eventually find a husband, but it was said to be a loveless arranged marriage that did nothing to help her forget the passionate affair of her youth.

The house built by John Hunt would see a series of different owners over the years. Eventually, it would be surrounded by other buildings, firmly part of Northampton, instead of on the city's outskirts. In 1900, Ruth Session would buy the building and turn it into a boardinghouse for Smith College students. Ruth Session knew about the secret entrance to the hidden room and loved to tell the girls who roomed at her house the story of the star-crossed lovers from the house's Revolutionary War days. In 1921, the school would buy the building outright and turn it into the dormitory it is today.

Students who live in Sessions House believe that in death, Johnnie Burgoyne has kept his promise to Lucy Hunt. The spirits of the lovers are supposed to be together and happy in Session House. They have also sparked a tradition of their own amongst the students who live with them.

This Halloween night tradition, started by the very first house mother of Sessions House after Smith bought the building, sends students who are new to the building on a search for the secret room. Upperclassmen keep the location a strictly held secret for just this reason. When a girl does discover the room, she is greeted inside by a senior who makes her swear to keep the location secret and then sends her off back to her room.

SPRINGFIELD COLLEGE

SPRINGFIELD

S pringfield College may not be the most haunted school in this book. And Springfield College's ghost may not be the scariest. But the school does have one unique claim to fame. In 1891, back when Springfield College was the International Young Men's Christian Association Training School, the sport of basketball was created and played for the first time. Dr. James Naismith, a professor at the school and fittingly the school's physical

education instructor, came up with the game on a rainy day while trying to find something to keep a notoriously rowdy class active and interested.

Needless to say, the game was a hit. The fact that it was perfectly suited for indoor play was key. New England's long and often unpredictable winters made the need for an indoor sport too important to be ignored. Dr. Naismith wrote up the basic rules of the game, nailed a peach basket to the wall, threw a soccer ball at his students and the rest, as they say, is history. The peach basket would morph into metal hoops and a backboard in 1906. The orange ball and, oddly enough, dribbling wouldn't be added to the game until the 1950s.

But Dr. James Naismith wouldn't live to see the now iconic orange ball be created. He passed away in 1939, nine days after suffering a major brain hemorrhage. Since nearly the moment of his death, Dr. Naismith's ghost has been spotted at Springfield College's Alumni Hall. He is said to look nearly identical to the way he did back on that day in 1891 when he nailed the first peach basket to the wall.

Dressed in an old-fashioned suit, vest carefully buttoned up beneath his blazer, Dr. Naismith watches over the college and all its students. Of course, he is said to take a particular interest in the basketball players. His spirit is most active on the third floor of the building, particularly Room 374, which was his own room at one point.

As time has gone on, more and more students report seeing the spirit without knowing who he was in life. In a real sign of the times, several have described him as wearing "Harry Potter glasses," without realizing the round lenses were very stylish in the early part of the 1900s.

STONEHILL COLLEGE

EASTON

Stonehill College is a private Roman Catholic school located in Easton, Massachusetts. The college is known for its happy students (ranked number seven in this category by the *Princeton Review*), for having accessible professors (number ten) and for the popularity of its intramural sports (number nine). Speaking of sports, the school's very popular athletic teams are called the Stonehill Skyhawks. The name is immensely more politically correct than the previous Native American–themed Chieftain name and also has ties to the very widely seen ghost that lives on campus.

While Stonehill College has many state-of-the-art buildings and is always growing, the campus itself sits on what was historically the Ames estate. During the nineteenth century, the Ames family was a prominent one in Massachusetts. Oliver Ames began the family's upward trajectory when he created the Ames Shovel Company. While the Ames family had long been making iron shovels, Oliver had the great fortune of making them just as gold rush fever gripped the country. Demand for shovels was as high as the demand for a gold-filled claim, and the Ames shovel was the preferred tool of choice. As the gold rush proved to be more of a gold bust, the shovel company continued to grow, this time supplying tools to the growing railroad industry. In time, the Ames family would take over interests in the railroads themselves, as well as becoming big in state politics. By the time the early 1900s rolled around, Oliver Ames's great-grandson Frederick would man the helm of the family empire. Frederick built a stunning fifty-room mansion in Easton, but he had a spirit for adventure that made it hard for him to stay tied down to the opulent home.

An early pioneer in the aviation field, Frederick Ames would found and act as president of Skyways, Inc., after graduating from Harvard University. Not the type to sit in his office, Frederick Ames made many flights in his own plane. After one North American tour, Ames stopped off in Mexico, where he would meet the love of his life, a French woman and renowned adventurer herself named Maurice Mozette. The couple eloped in Tucson, Arizona, and then took off for a wild honeymoon.

On their way back from this honeymoon, they would crash land at Ames's Easton estate, where he was well known for landing aircraft on his property. Luckily, the two newlyweds walked away from the crash totally unscathed. The Ames couple could most often be found flying between Easton and Boston, sometimes hopping in their plane just to go grab a bite to eat in the city. Eventually, Frederick Ames's high-flying antics would catch up to him. On one flight between Boston and his house, he missed his homemade landing strip and crashed into his own front lawn. Frederick Ames was killed instantly.

Popular legend blames the crash on a servant of Ames. This servant, tasked with staying up all night and lighting the edge of the runway so Ames could easily see it from the air, instead had a bit too much to drink and was passed out cold until the sound of the crash roused him. Other stories put the blame squarely on Ames's shoulders, saying he was flying inebriated and that, combined with his notorious daredevil risk-taking nature, led to his demise.

In time, Frederick Ames's widow would sell the fifty-room mansion with the detached gymnasium that featured a marble swimming pool and indoor tennis courts. Those two structures would become the first two buildings of the newly formed Stonehill College. The school opened in 1934 to an enrollment of just about 130 students.

Almost immediately, the ghost stories started cropping up among the student body. Since the school's earliest days, an unearthly blue mist is sometimes seen floating around the campus of Stonehill College. Described as vaguely diamond shaped, and roughly ten feet long, no natural cause has ever been found for the blue mist.

These kinds of spirits are well known in the halls of ghostly lore, but experts can't quite agree on why some ghosts appear as colored mists. One theory is that the blue mist is a kind of ectoplasm, which is one of the more rare paranormal occurrences. Another theory is that this kind of vaporous ghost is a pre-apparition. While the spirit has enough energy to manifest as more than just a cold spot, it is unable to fully form itself into the image of the person it once was.

It seems logical that the ghost seen on the campus of Stonehill College would be identified as that of Frederick Ames. Besides the fact that the land once belonged to Ames, and that it was the scene of his death, in life Ames had the kind of curious restless energy that could easily make one imagine that he lingers on after death, still roaming and adventuring.

It's also worth noting that Stonehill College, much like Bridgewater State University, which is featured in a chapter earlier in this book, falls into the northernmost corner of the Bridgewater Triangle. This famed paranormal hotspot located in southeastern Massachusetts has a whole host of reported activity, some of which is touched on in the Bridgewater State University chapter.

Stonehill College is located just on the outskirts of the wetlands area that was named Hockomock Swamp by the Wampanoag people who lived here long before the European settlers arrived in Massachusetts. Hockomock Swamp is considered, if not the geographic center of the mysterious Bridgewater Triangle, then certainly the heart of it. Appropriately enough, the name Hockomock means "the place where spirits dwell." When the European settlers arrived in this part of the state, they were much more direct when renaming the area, calling it "Devil's Swamp." Some stories say that the odd activity in this area comes from a Native American curse created by the Wampanoags' anger over the white settlers taking their land and destroying their traditional way of life. Others say the swamp has always been haunted and that the Native Americans both feared and revered it for this reason. The spirits that dwelled there could be evil, in Wampanoag mythos, or they could also be good spirits that led hunters to plentiful moose and deer.

While there have been plenty of ghost sightings in and around Hockomock Swamp, including that of a Native American man slowly rowing a homemade birch tree canoe through the murky waters, the dense wetlands are more well known for the strange animals that witnesses have reported seeing here over the years. These are all cryptid creatures. That is, they are animals that fall more under the interests of cryptozoologists than traditional biologists. Cryptids are creatures you are more likely to find in a book of myth and folklore than a science journal but whose existence is believed to be possible, by some, even while they are dismissed entirely by the established scientific community.

Even among firm believers of these kinds of creatures, the animals that have long been rumored to frequent Hockomock Swamp are...extreme. A long-standing story says that there are packs of dog-like creatures the size of ponies, with glowing red eyes no less, that live in the deepest parts of Hockomock Swamp. If the idea of two-hundred-pound dogs roaming freely through the largest freshwater swamp in Massachusetts and passing by with no scientific scrutiny at all seems wrong to you, never fear! Many people say these are phantom dogs, though what they are ghosts of is up for debate.

Giant devil dogs aside, there have been several sightings of a Sasquatch-like creature in Hockomock Swamp. The most famous of these occurred in 1978, when one Bridgewater resident by the name of Joe DeAndrade came across something he had never seen before as he stood with his back to Clay Banks, one of the small ponds that dot the outskirts of the swamp.

"I was standing there, and for some reason I had to turn around," DeAndrade told *Boston Globe* correspondent Ross Muscato in 2005 about the 1978 encounter. "It was a chill or something inside me. And I turned around, and there, off to the right, maybe two hundred yards away, there was this—well, I don't know what it was. It was a creature that was all brown and hairy, like a big apish-and-man thing. It was making its way for the woods, but I didn't stick around to watch where it was going. I ran for the street."

DeAndrade would return to the area again, this time armed with a camera and rifle, to try and track down the creature he saw that day. Neither DeAndrade nor the reinforcements he brought along with him ever found any proof of a large mammalian animal living in the swamp. But still, the man stuck to his story and even today insists that what he saw that day was something inexplicable.

Over the years, others have had brushes with creatures that seem to match the description of the one seen by Joe DeAndrade. Witnesses to the creature, which has become known as the Hockomock monster, include a muskrat trapper, two police officers and a local resident who says she saw something terrifying snacking on her backyard pumpkins one evening. Because the creature has been seen standing on its two hind legs, and running on all four, the skeptical have dismissed it as a rogue bear.

Those who have seen the creature with their own eyes remain unconvinced that what they saw was a bear. Many describe it as being more ape-like than bear-like. Most disturbingly, a lot of the witnesses say that when they drew at all close to the creature, it was surrounded by a wild dirty stench that was like nothing they had ever smelled before.

The idea of a sasquatch wandering around Massachusetts is probably a little easier to swallow than the thought of a devil dog—and certainly a pack of devil dogs. Recent studies by Angus Reid Public Opinion have found that in the United States, 29 percent of people say that Bigfoot "probably" or "definitely" exists. The same study looked at rates of belief in different famous cryptids like the Loch Ness Monster.

One of the creatures missing from the Angus Reid study, but not from the lore of Hockomock Swamp, was the thunderbird. Thunderbird is something of a catchall term in cryptozoology to describe any mysterious bird-like flying creature. These can range from something like a winged reptile to an oversized feathered bird and absolutely anything in between the two that you could imagine. While thunderbirds are not nearly as well known as sasquatch stories, reports of unexplainable flying creatures occur in nearly every culture dating back so far that they are closely tied to early myths from around the world. In fact, the thunderbird term itself is Native American in origin, and thunderbirds are an important part of the mythos of many tribes.

A pterodactyl-type creature with an eight-foot wingspan is among the many odd reports that sometimes lurch their way out of Hockomock Swamp. The people of the Wampanoag tribe who lived in this area of Massachusetts long before European settlers made their way here reported seeing it, and the same sorts of stories persist to this day. Before you go thinking that the thunderbird stories associated with Hockomock Swamp are just retellings of ancient Native American myths, you should know that there are a lot of modern-day accounts of sightings of this strange bird. One of these more modern reports came from none other than a Norton police sergeant named Thomas Downy. In 1971, Sergeant Downy was driving near a place at the edge of Hockomock Swamp that is known, appropriately enough, as Bird Hill when he saw a giant bird lift off into the sky. Sergeant Downy was so shaken up by the experience that he reported it. Because the report came from a fellow police officer, it was given a little more credence at the time than it would have been if reported by a random passerby. But though the police checked the area thoroughly, they could find no evidence of any creature of that size living in the area. Sargent Downy went on to be called the Birdman by his fellow officers for some time. Nevertheless, Downy stuck to his initial story.

If you're starting to think that Hockomock Swap sounds like a very unsafe place, you would be absolutely correct. But the real trouble isn't with the unexplainable creatures or possible ghosts. The real danger is the swamp itself. People can, and very often do, get lost in Hockomock Swamp. Unless you are a skilled outdoorsperson with a lot of knowledge of the area, ghost hunting in Hockomock Swamp is not recommended. Even longtime residents of the area have found themselves turned around in the swamp. One man and his dog went missing for an entire day in 2001; this happened despite the fact that the man had his cellphone on him and was in contact with his wife nearly the entire time and despite the efforts of dozens of volunteers and emergency personnel. At one point, a group of firefighters saw the missing man's fire, and they still couldn't reach him, driven back by the excessive vegetation and deep-sucking mud. While in the end the man, and his dog, came out of the fracas okay, it was only after calling in special rescue hovercraft that he could be reached.

University of Massachusetts–Lowell

CHELMSFORD

The main campus of the University of Massachusetts–Lowell has a great ghost story of its own, as you'll see in the next chapter, but the school's West Campus, located one town over in Chelmsford, Massachusetts, has ascended to near legendary status among the urban explorers and ghost hunters in the New England area. And this is despite the fact that very few people realize that UMASS Lowell even has a West Campus!

First, the bad news: no matter what you've heard about UMASS Lowell's mysteriously abandoned West Campus, it's just not true. The campus isn't abandoned at all. Sorry to be the one to break the news. Yes, there are several unused buildings on the small West Campus. But there is also one that is still very much in use. It's the main building just as you drive in; no way to sneak in around it or get into the West Campus and not be seen by absolutely everyone in and around the building before you make it to the decidedly abandoned buildings in the back. And yes, the people working in that still very much in use building know to watch out for any wannabe ghost hunters who come skulking about. Show up with an EMF reader and you will have the cops called on you so quickly your head will spin. For that matter, show up without an EMF reader and you're still likely to get hit with a trespassing charge. The buildings are dangerous. And the UMASS Lowell employees in the still-in-use building are completely sick of everyone always coming around trying to get to the rest of the campus.

Now, for the good news: everything *else* you've heard about West Campus is absolutely and completely true. It is a collection of half a dozen or so

The abandoned UMASS Lowell campus in Chelmsford is, according to local legend, as haunted as it looks.

Not every building on this campus is abandoned. Staff in this building have become de facto gate keepers, stopping exploration of the rest of the buildings behind it. No Trespassing signs abound.

The decay in and around the buildings make them unsafe for exploring.

buildings that look like they're straight out of a classic Hollywood movie about an old haunted school. They are filled with the softly decaying remnants of furniture, left behind as though someone was in a terrible rush to get out of there; they have smashed-out, boarded-up windows and graffiti warning of evil spirits and terrible deeds, and the front doors and window sills drip with overgrowth, creating shadowy places where anything could be hiding. And yes, this part is the best part of all: these buildings seem to be just as haunted as they look.

This collection of late 1800s and early 1900s brick buildings was not always part of a college campus, University of Massachusetts–Lowell or otherwise. It had a much more humble beginning as the Middlesex County Truant School for Boys. A collection of vintage photographs owned by Harvard University shows the truancy school in its heyday, the shrubs trimmed back carefully from the windows and the bricks still straight and whole. However, the history of the Middlesex Truant School for Boys is not well recorded. It is known that the school was authorized in 1892 as a home for habitually truant boys between the ages of seven and sixteen. In 1908, it was renamed with the slightly more positive sounding name Middlesex County Training School. It remained open until 1973. Outside of an article published in 1896 in the *Cambridge Chronicle* detailing the controversy of such places in their day, little is known of what life was like for the boys who were sent there by their towns back in the early part of the 1900s.

If the hauntings tell us anything about the Middlesex County Truant School for Boys, it is that it was more a place of punishment than one of learning or reform. Today, ghostly screams emanate loudly from the

Originally used as a truancy school in the 1800s, the buildings remained in use until the 1970s.

abandoned buildings, and an air of sadness and pain radiates from this place. While UMASS Lowell goes to sometimes extreme lengths to keep the curious off the West Campus, there are those who will swear that they have not only made it into the compound but also into the abandoned buildings themselves.

They tell stories of water-logged rooms with broken-up desks and children's toys scattered around here and there, broken light fixtures falling from the ceilings in a wave of dead wires, mold growing gaily up the stained and filthy walls. Inside the buildings, it's like walking on sponges, fun house floors that roil and creak with each footfall, and shadows abound everywhere. Even if there didn't appear to be some very active spirits in this place, it would be easy enough for the mind's imagination to conjure up more than a few.

West Campus's Gould Hall is home to a particularly nasty haunt. The building has been carefully boarded up, but stories of Gould Hall's haunted nature have been dispersed enough that people keep finding new ways to get in. Of course, when it comes to abandoned buildings, ghosts aren't the only draw. One group of teens disregarded the ghost stories in hopes of finding a secluded place to party and got more than they bargained for.

From almost the first moment Melissa saw Gould Hall, she knew she didn't want to go inside. She'd never seen such a downright creepy looking

place in her entire life. And that was just the from the walkway by the front stairs. The thought of actually going inside, being trapped inside the middle of the brick beast, sent shivers up her spine and made her feel sick to her stomach. But no one else in the group seemed to feel as scared as she did by the building, and she didn't want to be the one to call the whole thing off. It

Gould Hall is among the most haunted of the UMASS Lowell abandoned West Campus buildings.

was silly, anyway. They'd already been inside two of the other buildings on West Campus, and it had been fine. Well, dirty and wet, but nothing scary. Her group of friends wanted to find a comfortable place to sit for a while and hang out. Gould Hall was the next building they stumbled across, and despite the graffiti outside warning them off, they decided it couldn't be any worse than Read Hall or Ipswich Hall before it had been.

Inside, Gould Hall didn't look much different than those other two had. Same mold, dirt and debris. But it just felt terrible. Melissa couldn't shake the feeling that they weren't alone in the building. She kept feeling fingers poking at her and running up and down her skin. At one point, she turned quickly, starting to yell, convinced that a man was behind her touching her long blond hair.

She realized she couldn't breathe. The air was oppressive. The rest of her friends seemed to feel the same. Where before they had laughed and joked as they explored the condemned buildings of West Campus, in Gould Hall they now spoke in whispers and walked close together, glancing endlessly back and forth into dark corners and down hallways, convinced that something would come out of the darkness at them.

"Let's get out of here," Melissa finally said out loud, trying—and failing—to sound casual and bored.

Graffiti warning explorers of the dark presence inside Gould Hall.

She saw a few of her friends nod their heads, and then everyone turned to leave. The only problem was that everyone turned in different directions. Melissa suddenly realized that she couldn't remember which way they had come in either. Everyone grabbed hands so they couldn't get separated in the dark gloom of the building and started walking down random hallways and into rooms she could have sworn they didn't pass coming in. Even though Gould Hall wasn't very large—in fact, it was one of the smaller ones on West Campus—Melissa and her friends walked for what seemed like hours and couldn't find their way out.

Melissa figured it was nerves clouding her judgment, but she couldn't figure out why no one in the group recognized anything they were walking past. She felt dizzy and sick and couldn't shake the feeling that she was being watched by something that hated them but wouldn't let them go. She tried checking her phone to see how long they'd been trapped inside the building, but she couldn't get it to turn on. Her friends had the same problem, and one pointed out that his wristwatch had stopped as well. Finally, she suggested they break a window and risk someone hearing the noise. She was willing to do anything to get out of the building. Seeing the flashing lights of a police car right about now would have been a relief no matter how much trouble they would get into later.

As Melissa's friend approached the window, part of a chair in hand to help him pry the plywood away, a strange glow started in a corner of the room and flew violently at them. Everyone screamed and ran. Instantly, they found themselves at the door they'd used to get inside; they couldn't explain why it had been so hard to find just a minute before.

Other buildings at UMASS Lowell's abandoned West Campus might not be quite as terrifyingly haunted as Gould Hall, but they all seem to have

at least a small assortment of tales and spooks wandering around their decaying hallways. Other clandestine explorers have lived to tell the tale of being pelted with old children's toys as they stumbled around the filthy rooms or feeling as if they walked into a freezing cold force field that drove their iPods and cellphones wild—or kept them from starting up at all. One of the buildings has what looks like the remains of a haphazard basketball court out back, and yes, there are reports of people hearing the ghostly sound of a very competitive game.

Directly behind the abandoned school is a recently built development of residential houses. The people who live here have called the local police more than once because of the strange noises they sometimes hear coming from the buildings. But it's hard to say if they're hearing ghosts or hearing the many trespassers who try to make their way into the buildings of West Campus. At the center of the campus, there have sometimes been reports of a wild light display, an eerie glow that has been likened to being closer to an aurora borealis than kids with flashlights.

UNIVERSITY OF MASSACHUSETTS–LOWELL

LOWELL

U niversity of Massachusetts–Lowell's main campus might not have the ultra-creepy architecture of its long rumored, and surprisingly very real, West Campus in Chelmsford, but that doesn't mean that you won't find some ghosts there. In fact, there is one ghost at UMASS Lowell that takes creepy to a whole new level.

Coulrophobia is the scientific name for fear of clowns. And as silly as it might seem to someone who doesn't have this particular phobia, it really is no laughing matter (pun most definitely intended). Clowns, no matter how humorous they seem to anyone else, can induce sweating, nausea, an increased heartbeat, tears and an extreme feeling of dread in someone suffering from coulrophobia. And before you start thinking this particular fear besets only a small segment of society, keep in mind that the fear is so widespread that one study done by England's University of Sheffield in 2008 concluded that clowns were "universally disliked by children."

But coulrophobia doesn't just strike the young. Many people carry that fear with them well into adulthood. Some will point to a run-in with a creepy clown as a child as the start of their fear. Others credit Pennywise, the main adversary in Stephen King's bestselling novel *It*, as the granddaddy of all terrifying clowns. But most seem to have no idea where the phobia has come from. Bestival, a three-day-long music festival held annually in England, has had to ask attendees to not dress as clowns out of respect to the large portion of the audience who described themselves as being very disturbed by clowns.

Bourgeois Hall is one of two haunted buildings on the UMASS Lowell campus.

But even those who have never had an adverse reaction to a clown in their life might think twice after coming face to face with the ghost at UMASS Lowell's Leitch Hall. This residency building, as austere and institutional looking as a dorm could be, is said to be haunted by a ghost clown.

That's right. A ghost dressed as a clown. Red nose, colorful oversized pants, white face makeup and all. Still laughing? It gets even creepier. The ghost tends to wait until the building is nearly empty, during school breaks or RA training, and then walks up and down the hallways knocking on the doors. Those who have heard the ghost knocking report seeing the fully made-up clown figure hovering outside the door. Those who are brave enough to open the door and accost the clown say he disappears without a trace before they can confront him.

Leitch Hall stands directly across a walkway from a nearly identical structure named Bourgeois Hall, which is also a dormitory building. Bourgeois Hall is safe from roaming ghostly clowns, at least as far as anyone can tell. But it is supposed to be connected to Leitch Hall by an underground tunnel. And this tunnel is the home to a very loud and unhappy ghost. Despite the fact that the tunnel was sealed up years ago, many students complain of loud groaning and clanking coming from the space where the tunnel is supposed to connect the two buildings.

Leitch Hall, directly across a walkway from Bourgeois Hall, shares a similar-looking structure and haunting with the other dorm building.

How likely is it that there is a tunnel connecting these two buildings that are located so very close to each other to begin with? There's actually a pretty good chance that something like a tunnel may have existed at some point. Many Massachusetts colleges and universities once featured these kinds of tunnels so students could move easily around campus even during bouts of New England's famously temperamental weather. Eames Hall, another of UMASS Lowell's residency buildings, has a tunnel of its own that connects it to the Southwick Food Court located directly across the street. This tunnel is still currently in use by students, though there's no ghost story to be found attached to it.

WELLESLEY COLLEGE

WELLESLEY

It's a long-standing tradition at this private Seven Sisters college in Wellesley, Massachusetts, that each Halloween the public is invited to climb the steps of the haunted Galen Stone Tower. Along the way, they are assaulted by giant spiders, white-sheet ghosts and haunting Halloween-themed music. At the top of the tower, guests get a magnificent view of the Wellesley College campus and a look at the tower's thirty-two solid bronze bells. The event is hosted by the Guild of Carillonneurs, a student organization that holds the honor of being one of the few student-run bodies in the country to play their school's carillon instead of it being under the auspices of a professional carillonneur.

It's a popular Halloween event that many in the community come to enjoy year after year. The fact that the Galen Stone Tower isn't haunted in the slightest does nothing to dampen the raucous Halloween spirit. But just because the tower isn't haunted doesn't mean that there aren't ghosts to be found elsewhere on Wellesley College's beautiful five-hundred-acre campus.

The Diana Chapman Walsh Alumnae Hall is thought to be the real place to go when it comes to spooks at Wellesley College. It probably helps that the building is home to not just

one but two theaters. The main theater, the Barstow Auditorium, is a 1,300-seat Beaux-Arts beauty that was given an $18 million facelift in 2010.

Theater director Nora Hussey first became aware of the Barstow's spirit when she noticed a student onstage during a rehearsal leaning awkwardly to stare into the empty seats of the auditorium. When she took the student aside to see what the problem was, the young actress was insistent that she had seen a man in a dark suit watching the rehearsal. Hussey knew beyond a doubt that the theater was empty at the time and passed it off as nerves or a trick of the light. She was forced to revisit her initial explanation and reassess it after hearing similar accounts over the years from students who all described in careful detail the same dark-suited man, in a very outlandish top hat, who liked to watch them rehearse.

While this might sound like a pretty innocuous spirit, some have credited him with a darker side. These witnesses have seen him in military garb rather than his suit. The few who have seen both the suited man and the man in a World War I uniform swear it is the same figure just in different clothes. As the war veteran, he puts off a more malignant energy and seems less concerned with watching the show than he is with upsetting the actors. Some have claimed to feel sudden pinches or slaps, leading to speculation that it's the ghost's way of critiquing the show or the performances of the cast.

One former student, a current military helicopter pilot, which gives some credence to witness accounts that she normally has nerves of steel, was backstage one evening. Earlier in the day, another student had claimed to see the military man, but she had never given much thought to the ghost stories before. She'd been backstage by herself before and never had any problems. Suddenly, a pillar of cold air seemed to descend rapidly from the ceiling, centering on the young woman. Besides being suddenly frozen, the student said she felt a wave of boiling anger emanating from the air around her. She decided to take it as a warning and, with some effort, pulled herself from the enveloping cold and fled the theater. After that, she took the ghost stories more seriously and refused to be backstage by herself again.

The top-hatted military man isn't the only ghost in the theater. Luckily for the people who spend a lot of time in the theater, there is a more comforting spirit that is said to haunt the Barstow Auditorium. This is Paul Barstow, who acted as theater director and chairman of the Theater Department at Wellesley College for over forty years. The auditorium is named in his honor. Nora Hussey, the current theater director, says she has had as many run-ins with Paul's spirit as students have had with the dark-suited man. In the fall of 2004, the Theater Department did a small production in honor of Paul

Barstow's life. As the finale song began, a dazzling light show started up, pulsing in time with the music, "Let the Sun Shine."

It was a completely unplanned and unrehearsed display that was pulled off without a hitch. As they were leaving, many theatergoers expressed how stunned they were by the finale. As she was leaving the show herself, Nora went to the sound booth to thank the lighting technician for the extra arrangement he had pulled off without her knowledge. It had been a marvelous surprise.

Nora Hussey found Ken Loewit, the technician, standing outside the booth paled faced and shaking. Before she could say a word, he looked up at her surprised face and told her, "I swear, I didn't touch a single control."

Such a spectacular display has not been seen again in the Barstow Auditorium since the finale of the Paul Barstow play. Nora Hussey swears she believes it was the spirit of Paul Barstow putting his final touch and stamp of approval on the production.

Beneath the Barstow Auditorium is a smaller black box theater in part of what used to be an old ballroom. This theater is haunted by Rob, who has an interesting and very unique Wellesley College pedigree. In 1992, the black box theater put on a production of *Lady Bird, Lady Bird*. The play was written by William Rough about his mother, a Wellesley College graduate, who was one of the original barnstorming aviatrixes along with Amelia Earhart. The play included a relatively minor character named Rob that, upon staging and rehearsals, just didn't quite work for the production. The character was cut, and the play suffered none for it, though the exclusion sparked off odd occurrences at the theater ever since.

The night of the first showing of *Lady Bird, Lady Bird*, things went off without a hitch. That is, without a hitch until the very end, when the light and soundboard went crazy. The technician was perplexed. She was very familiar with the equipment and had never had a problem with it before. As the run of *Lady Bird, Lady Bird* continued, the problems persisted, though no one could find an electrical problem that explained the suddenly unmanageable equipment.

Eventually, *Lady Bird, Lady Bird* made its way to the Barstow Auditorium upstairs. While no light or sound problems had ever occurred up there before, as soon as that particular play started, the same problems that had become common during its run in the black box theater showing started up in the Barstow Auditorium.

It is unclear how students got the idea that Rob, the character cut from the play, was somehow the problem. In time, people learned to hang small model biplanes inside the sound and light booth at the black box theater, and that seemed to help calm down the odd occurrences. Some productions have gone so far as to thank the mysterious Rob in their playbooks, and this seems to please the spirit very much.

WESTERN NEW ENGLAND UNIVERSITY

SPRINGFIELD

The name Western New England University has been around for only the past few years. Previously, the college was called Western Massachusetts College. The school is located on a sprawling 215-acre campus in Springfield, Massachusetts. Its nearly four thousand students are housed across ten college dormitories, two of which have had some unusual activity reported by students. Interestingly, both the haunted rooms in the

Western New England University campus seem to be a little more dangerous than your average college haunt, though no connection has yet been found between them.

Students who are assigned to Room 401 in Berkshire Hall find out very quickly that they are not alone in their room. Night after night, they are awakened by the alarming sound of breaking glass. When they get up to investigate the noise, they find they can't. Somehow they are being held in place by some kind of unseen force. The crushing weight of this energy keeps them from calling out for help and produces the panicky feeling of being unable to breathe. Usually after a few moments, the feeling subsides, but that does little to calm the trepidation of those who have experienced it.

Room 133 in Windham Hall is a less alarming space, but not by much. Instead of brief moments where they brush against the darker side of the afterlife, students in this room have the constant feeling of being watched. While being tracked by this presence they cannot see, students feel unable to get warm, no matter what the temperature in the room is supposed to be. The constant chill people report in this room can't be tracked by thermometers, but student after student has trekked down to the maintenance department to complain of the constant cold.

Those who spend a lot of time in this room seem to get sicker more often than their fellow students. They're sick and exhausted and don't know why.

Churchill Hall may be haunted by a former librarian or book lover.

Either the constant cold wears them down or the watchful presence drains them of their energy.

Churchill Hall on the Western New England University campus has an interesting history. For many years before its renovations, it housed the campus library. Today, among other things, it houses a computer lab. There's at least one long-term resident at the university that refuses to accept this change.

"She doesn't have a name," Kelly says earnestly. "No one knows who she is. But there's definitely something there."

Kelly believes the ghost at Churchill Hall could be that of a former librarian. On more than one occasion, she's gone back to her dorm room after a night at the computer lab to find that whatever novel she was in the middle of reading was mysteriously missing from her backpack. After retracing her steps a few times, she would find the book, again and again, open halfway and tucked into various corners of the Churchill Hall building.

"I swear, it looked just like I'd interrupted someone who was reading it," she elaborated. "Like they heard me coming to look for it so they tossed it down and hid."

After a while, whenever one of her books went missing, she'd head straight for Churchill Hall to find it, no more searching her bag or car or trying to remember where she had it last. The books were always in Churchill Hall. Another student, upon hearing of Kelly's missing book troubles and her

belief that a dedicated reader was haunting Churchill Hall, told her that while she had never had books go missing, she had some strange experiences in the building, too.

During her own time, after her schoolwork was done, this student liked to sit in Churchill Hall with a yellow legal pad, her headphones on and a cup of coffee while she worked on what she hoped would one day turn into her first novel. She liked the quietness of the building for writing. But after a few trips, the quietness started to grate on her. She felt convinced that someone was standing behind her even when she knew she was alone in the room.

She started writing sans headphones, hoping that if she could hear there was no one there it would help calm her nerves. No luck. The more she wrote in Churchill Hall, the more she felt watched. Then things started to escalate. Where once before she'd felt only the presence around her, after being there a while, she started to feel as though someone was hovering over her as soon as she walked into the building.

While she never felt threatened by whatever it was, the feeling unnerved her. It certainly didn't help her concentrate on her writing. She found a new spot on campus to pursue her writing hobby. Whatever the feeling was, she never felt it anywhere else on campus, but the feeling persisted any time she had reason to step inside Churchill Hall.

WESTFIELD STATE UNIVERSITY

WESTFIELD

S ure, I lived in the haunted dorm room," Bill said, smiling casually, obviously having said this line many times before. "But it's not haunted anymore."

Bill was being a little disingenuous. While Westfield State University has, or had, a well-known and very active spirit within its Davis Hall dormitory, the spirit was linked to a supply closet and not a dorm room at all. Popular legend in the town of Westfield says that a student at the school hanged himself in his room over Thanksgiving break. But the room at the center of the ghost stories is a top-floor supply closet.

"I never saw the ghost, but I sort of had an experience one time with it," a girl named Ashley broke in. She looked shyly at Bill. "I was in Davis and passed a girl in the hallway, I didn't know her well, but I had a few classes with her here and there. Anyway, she had a look on her face that made me think, 'Damn, she looks like she's seen a ghost.' And then she grabbed me and said she had! I almost thought I had said what I was thinking out loud!"

The girl told Ashley she had just passed the hazy specter of a darkly handsome young man leaning against the wall. As she approached the figure, a wave of cold air hit her so hard she stumbled. At the same time, she was gripped with a feeling of despair she could not explain. She reached out to touch the boy, trying to figure out what was going on, and he winked out of existence. It wasn't like in a movie where he slowly faded away. Just one instant he was there, and the next it was as if nothing had ever been.

A few minutes later, she was rushing down the hall, and that's when she stumbled into Ashley. The girls went together to see if the apparition was still there. Ashley didn't see the ghost, or feel the blast of cold air, but as she reached for the doorknob of the supply closet that the young man had been standing next to, she found herself unable to force herself to open it. She felt chills through her hands, but she couldn't say if it was feelings that were being evoked by the ghost or just her own overactive imagination getting to her. She didn't think she believed in ghosts, but everyone said this closet on this floor was haunted, and the other girl seemed so sure of what she had seen.

Later, after a few weeks had passed and she was able to start to cast some doubt in her own mind over what had really happened that day, she approached the closet again. This time, she was able to grasp the doorknob and fling the door open no problem. She was greeted with bright yellow buckets used for mopping and some unlabeled bottles of cleaning supplies. The only odd thing, as far as she could tell, was that it looked as if the closet was painted entirely black.

In time, Ashley would meet a lot of students who claimed to have seen or felt the ghost. Many residents of Davis Hall would tell friends that they lived in the very room where a student had killed himself. It certainly made a better story to say that you lived in a haunted room than to say that you lived in a dorm with a haunted janitor's closet. It wasn't too strange to see groups of students making the trek to the supply closet in hopes of catching their own glimpse of this unnamed ghost.

Eventually, either out of the need to suppress the ghost stories or just annual maintenance, Westfield State University repainted the supply closet. This time, it picked a less unusual color for the walls. Since that time, there have been no reports of ghostly activity, though many students still wander over to that part of the building in hopes of seeing the ghost.

While it may seem like an odd way to get rid of a ghost, repainting wasn't a bad idea on the part of the school. Ghosts seem to not like home renovations. Many people swear their house was never haunted until they started rearranging the furniture. Even something as simple as tearing down old wallpaper has sparked some hauntings. Many ghosts are attached to their homes; something emotional occurred there that keeps them lingering on. They get upset when living people start meddling with what they see as "their" home. Other ghosts have so little energy that they fall dormant for years. Sudden renovations stir up old emotions and energies. Either the ghost is unhappy with the work being done and feels the sudden urge to let the new owners know its opinion, or it is so excited that the home is being lived in that it is invigorated. Paranormal experts usually tell clients in these situations to talk to their ghosts. Explaining what changes are being made and why placates many unhappy spirits. Why the ghost of Davis Hall seemed tied to the paint color in the supply closet is unknown, but it will be interesting to see if he pops back up a few years down the road when the closet is painted again.

WHEATON COLLEGE

NORTON

What do Prince Shad Al-Sherif Pasha of the Hijaz and Turkey, former New Jersey governor Christine Todd Whitman and HBO executive Elaine Meryl Brown all have in common? They are all alumni of Wheaton College, a private four-year college located approximately halfway between Boston and Providence in the town of Norton, Massachusetts.

The school began in 1834 as a female seminary. There are at least two charming school traditions that date back to those days. In the 1800s, it was common to see young couples walking around Wheaton College's picturesque Peacock Pond in the early days of their courting. A long-standing tradition at the school says that if a young man walked a girl around the pond on three separate occasions and didn't kiss her, she was obligated to shove him in or she would suffer bad luck in her pursuit of a future husband. Another tradition at Wheaton College was that on graduation day, the first girl to touch the statue of Hebe, which stands outside Metcalf and Kilham Halls, would be the first of her graduating class to be married. Since the school opened up to men in the late 1980s, these marriage traditions have been, more or less, abandoned.

Besides pond-soaked lovers wandering the campus, there are a number of ghosts at Wheaton College. Many of these also date back to the college's time as an all-girls' school and the search for a suitable husband. Legend tells of a girl named Susan who went to such extreme lengths to see her boyfriend that she arranged a secret rendezvous for the two of them on the roof of the Mary Lyon Building. Unfortunately, the weather was not on

Susan's side. Once on the roof, the two were so cold that Susan left to get a blanket from her dorm for them to share. On her way back to her dorm, she was stopped by the headmaster, who followed her back to her room and stayed outside all night to make sure she wouldn't be sneaking around campus again that evening. Susan's boyfriend bore the real consequences of his girlfriend getting caught. Left atop the roof, legend says, he froze to death while he waited for her to come back with the blanket.

Looking at the building today, it's hard to say where exactly the couple was supposed to be having their clandestine meeting. The entire roof is fully exposed to anyone walking by and is, honestly, rather steep. The legend would be slightly more believable if it specified a secret way the two could have found into the cupola on top of the Greek Revival–style building. While there are certainly some problems with the legend itself, the need to invent such a story is more than apparent to any student at Wheaton College who has wandered into the ghost of the Mary Lyon Building.

Said to be that of a young man, the ghost is often seen floating aimlessly around the halls and rooms inside the building. For a ghost said to have died on the roof, he spends a lot of time walking up and down the interior stairs. Interestingly, the Mary Lyon Building was the site of a rather extensive fire in 1878. Just before the building was completed, this fire broke out in the basement. This was during the early morning hours, and it was thanks solely to a breakfast cook with the habit of coming into work extra early that that the blaze was contained before it consumed the entire building. Nearly all of the newly constructed building was saved, but many who came to fight the blaze were overcome with smoke inhalation. The burnt beams of this building can still be seen down in the Mary Lyon Building basement. Contemporary records do not specify if anyone died in the fire or while fighting it. There's at least a small chance that the ghost of the Mary Lyon Building is linked to this fire and not to a tale of love found and lost on the building's roof.

Another tale of love gone terribly wrong at Wheaton College takes place in Everett Hall. In the late 1920s, not long after the building was dedicated, there was a young female resident who flaunted the rules and often had her boyfriend come up to her room. The boyfriend was known for his temper, and the bad vibe he put out was enough to stop the other students from turning him in to campus officials. One night, the boyfriend's temper flared up and, during a loud argument with his girlfriend, got violent. Terrified, the girl fled from her room and dashed for the stairs. In her haste to get away from him, she slipped on the top step and fell, breaking her neck.

Today, there is a ghost in Everett Hall associated with this tragic tale. Luckily, it's not the spirit of the angry boyfriend. Beginning in 1939, after the school repainted the stairwells, the ghost sightings began. For many students, the spirit is simply an unseen presence, a feeling of being watched when no one is there, a cold spot on an otherwise warm day. Others say they have felt icy cold hands grip their arms or shoulders when they stumble on the stairs. A few have even seen the figure of a crying girl in old-fashioned clothes floating up and down the stairs that are supposed to have taken her life nearly one hundred years before.

Not every ghost at Wheaton College is that of a young girl unlucky in love. There are at least two others that linger on because their dedication to the school is stronger than life and death. One is that of Reverend Dr. Samuel Cole. Cole took up presidency at the college in 1897, long before the school evolved from being a female seminary to gaining its charter as a four-year college. Cole was behind a great deal of expansion on campus and remained president until his death in 1925.

One of the buildings that Cole saw built in his time at Wheaton College would go on to bear his name. A year after his death, the Cole Memorial Chapel was dedicated in his honor. And appropriately enough, this chapel is supposed to house his spirit. Samuel Cole is said to play tricks with the lights—he tends to like them dimmed—and to enjoy playing the sound system at night when the chapel is supposed to be empty. Many students tell the stories about walking past the brick building to hear eerie noises and unexplained music wafting out.

The other spirit whose love for the school keeps her tied to it is Mary Brown. Mary Brown spent most of her life as head librarian at the school, and instead of passing on when she died, she still shows up for work each and every day.

"I saw something once," John, a former security guard at the school admitted, a bit sheepishly. "I don't like to say I saw the ghost, but I definitely saw something."

Being a public safety officer at a school like Wheaton College is, most of the time, a fairly boring job. The campus is brightly lit and very safe, and the students, for the most part, don't get up to too much trouble. Then one night, while on his usual rounds, John saw a dark figure enter the elevator in the closed, and locked, library. Figuring students had broken in, maybe for a prank but possibly with something more sinister in mind, he quickly entered the building and stopped the elevator. Though it hadn't had time to stop at another floor and let off any passengers, the elevator was empty. Just to be sure, he combed through the entire building trying to catch whomever he had seen. No one was there.

While the security officer didn't find his prowler, he did find something else that was much more unusual. There was a stack of books, very neatly piled, standing in one of the walkways between the bookshelves. It wasn't just that the library staff was usually so good about picking up after students before closing for the night. The stack of books was, John estimated, about seven feet tall and would have required the use of a ladder to create. John went back to his original assumption. It had to be some kind of prank. But he couldn't figure out why the prowler was stacking books or how he or she had slipped past him in the building.

Library staff could have told him that oddly placed books was nothing strange. Mary Brown seems to spend a lot of the evening hours reshelving. Opening staff often finds books she was known to love in life laying open on the circulation desk in the morning.

BIBLIOGRAPHY

Abeel, Daphne. "Avon Hill: A Rose by Any Other Name." *Cambridge Historian*, September 2012. http://cambridgehistory.org/discover/newsletters/chronicle-fall-2012.pdf.

Angus Reid Public Opinion. "Americans More Likely to Believe in Bigfoot than Canadians." March 4, 2012. http://www.angus-reid.com/polls/44419/americans-more-likely-to-believe-in-bigfoot-than-canadians.

Bair, Diane, and Pamela Wright. "Tales from the Dark Side of Massachusetts."*BostonGlobe.com*. October 28, 2012. http://www.bostonglobe.com/lifestyle/travel/2012/10/27/tales-from-dark-side-massachusetts/vEC0iwI2DVgOFIIrcQ8GaJ/story.html.

Balzano, Christopher. "Haunted Tradition: Ghosts, Legends and Tradition at Smith College." *Mass Crossroads*. 2005. http://www.masscrossroads.com/session.

Bardsley, Marilyn. "The Boston Stranglers." *Boston Strangler*. Crime Library on TruTV.com http://www.trutv.com/library/crime/serial_killers/notorious/boston/21.html.

Belanger, Jeff. *Our Haunted Lives: True Life Ghost Stories*. Franklin Lakes, NJ: New Page, 2006.

Belanger, Jeff, Mark Moran and Mark Sceurman. *Weird Massachusetts: Your Travel Guide to the Bay State's Local Legends and Best Kept Secrets*. New York: Sterling, 2008.

Boston Fire Historical Society, and Stephanie Schorow. *Boston's Fire Trail*. Charleston, SC: The History Press, 2007.

Brancatella, Caroline. "Haunted Heights: BC Ghost Story Rumors Remain Vague." *The Heights*. October 22, 2001. Web. http://www.bcheights.com/2.6176/haunted-heights-bc-ghost-story-rumors-remain-vague-1.927600.

———. "Scary Stories Scarce at Boston College." *The Heights*. October 23, 2000. http://www.bcheights.com/2.6178/scary-stories-scarce-at-bc-1.929809#.UUiTYhyG0Qo.

Briggs, Bill. "No Laughing Matter: Fear of Clowns Is Serious Issue." *NBC News*. April 20, 2012. http://bodyodd.nbcnews.com/_news/2012/04/20/11268831-no-laughing-matter-fear-of-clowns-is-serious-issue?lite.

Brown, Edward A. "Haunted BU Eugene O'Neil." *BU Today*. September 29, 2009. http://www.bu.edu/today/2009/haunted-by-eugene-o'neill.

Cambridge Chronicle. "Middlesex County Truant School." February 1, 1896. http://cambridge.dlconsulting.com/cgi-bin/cambridge?a=d.

Charlesgate Hotel Ghost Stories. "Charlesgate Hotel: Ghost Stories & Haunted Folklore." Celebrate Boston. http://www.celebrateboston.com/ghost/charlesgate-hotel-ghost.htm.

Chestnut, Debi. "5 Reasons Your Home May Be Haunted." *Llewellyn Worldwide*. http://www.llewellyn.com/journal/article/2227.

Coleman, Loren. *Mysterious America: The Ultimate Guide to the Nation's Weirdest Wonders, Strangest Spots, and Creepiest Creatures*. New York: Paraview Pocket, 2007.

Daily Free Press. "Babe Ruth, Boston Strangler May Haunt Dorms." October 31, 2003. http://dailyfreepress.com/2003/10/31/babe-ruth-boston-strangler-may-haunt-dorms.

Danahy, Lauren. "Haunted Places on the North Shore." *Endicott College*. September 21, 2009. http://www.endicott.edu/Media/Attachments/Endicott/attachmentsadmin/1/HauntedPlacesontheNorthShore1009.pdf.

Faust, Drew. "Houses at Harvard College." *Harvard University*. 2011. http://www.fas.harvard.edu/home/content/houses-harvard-college.

Felix, W. "BSU Ghost Stories." *BSU Commuter Services Blog*. October 28, 2011. http://bsucommutes.com/halloween/bsu-ghost-stories.

Forest, Christopher. *Boston's Haunted History: Exploring the Ghosts and Graves of Beantown*. Atglen, PA: Schiffer Pub., 2008.

———. *North Shore Spirits of Massachusetts*. Atglen, PA: Schiffer Pub., 2009.

Fusco, C.J. *Old Ghosts of New England: A Traveler's Guide to the Spookiest Sites in the Northeast*. Woodstock, VT: Countryman, 2009.

Gawlik, Stephen. "Stepping Inside Boston College's Legendary House of Mystery." *Boston College*. http://www.bc.edu/bc_org/rvp/pubaf/chronicle/v11/o31/oconnell.html.

Gellerman, Bruce, and Erik Sherman. *Boston Curiosities*. Guilford, CT: Globe Pequot, 2010.

Goodwin, Nicholas. *Spooky Creepy Boston*. Atglen, PA: Schiffer Pub. Ltd., 2010.

"Halloween Feature: Lost on Gallows' Hill." *Cambridge.gov*. http://www2. cambridgema.gov/historic/halloween2.html.

Harrisson Weir, Emily. "Grave Concerns and Tall Tales." *On the Edge*, December 1996. https://www.mtholyoke.edu/offices/comm/vista/9612/6.html.

Harvard Crimson. "The Ghosts of Harvard." January 15, 1997. http://www. thecrimson.com/article/1997/1/15/the-ghosts-of-harvard-pbtbhe-yard.

Hauck, Dennis William. *Haunted Places: The National Directory: Ghostly Abodes, Sacred Sites, UFO Landings, and Other Supernatural Locations*. New York: Penguin, 2002.

"The Haunting of Salem State College." *Haunt in Salem State College*. January 28, 2011. http://www.hauntin.gs/Salem-State-College-Salem-State-University-North-Campus_Salem_Massachusetts_United-States_5448.

Huffington Post. "13 Haunted Campuses." October 29, 2010. Web. http://www. huffingtonpost.com/2010/10/29/13-haunted-campuses_n_775428. html#s165433&title=Boston_University_Shelton.

Kuong, Richard S. "Hometown Hauntings." *Wellesley Weston Online*. 2006. http://www.wellesleywestonmagazine.com/fall06/haunting.htm.

Lee, Sharon. "The Big Foot Phenomena." *Cryptomundo*, September 19, 2012. http://www.cryptomundo.com/bigfoot/bigfoot-is-real.

"The Legend of the Widow's Walk." *Waymarking.com*. http://www.waymarking. com/waymarks/WM5385_The_Legend_of_the_Widows_Walk.

Loomer, Jennifer, and Katherine Underwood. "Traditions: Founders Day Ice Cream." *Mount Holyoke College*. September 2003. https://www.mtholyoke. edu/courses/rschwart/hatlas/traditions/fdicecream.htm.

"Mark and Phillis Executions, 1755." *CelebrateBoston.com*. http://www. celebrateboston.com/crime/puritan-mark-and-phillis-executions.htm.

"MHC Ghost Story to Air on Travel Channel." *Mount Holyoke College*. October 22, 2004. https://www.mtholyoke.edu/offices/comm/csj/102204/ghost.shtml.

Morton, R.M. "The Ghosts of Bridgewater State University." *BSU Campus Center Blog RSS*. October 27, 2010. http://rccblog.com/2010/10/27/ ghostsofbsu-2.

Muscato, Ross A. "Easton's Spooky, Scary and Downright Frightful Past and Present—Easton, MA Patch." *Easton Patch*, October 29, 2010. http:// easton-ma.patch.com/articles/eastons-spooky-scary-and-downright-frightful-past-and-present.

————. "The Hockomock Swamp—Beautiful and Dangerous—Easton, MA Patch." *Easton Patch*, April 6, 2011. http://easton-ma.patch.com/articles/the-hockomock-swamp-beautiful-and-dangerous.

————. "Tales from the Swamp." *Boston.com*. October 30, 2005. http://www.boston.com/news/local/articles/2005/10/30/tales_from_the_swamp.

Plumb, Taryn. "Is Anyone There?" *Boston.com*. January 29, 2012. http://www.boston.com/news/local/articles/2012/01/29/hunting_ghosts_in_groveland_is_latest_college_course_offering.

Reading [Pennsylvania] *Eagle*. "4 Die, 25 Inured in Boston Hotel Fire." March 29, 1963.

"Real-World Haunted Houses: 5 Spooktacular Boston Spots." *Boston.com*. October 30, 2011. http://www.boston.com/lifestyle/blogs/thenextgreatgeneration/2011/10/real-world_haunted_houses_5_sp.html.

Ripich, Amy N. "Fearsome Phantoms Lurking in the Ivy." *Harvard Crimson*, October 31, 1986. http://www.thecrimson.com/article/1986/10/31/fearsome-phantoms-lurking-in-the-ivy.

Savdie, Nicole. "Thayer and Its Friendly Ghost." *Harvard Crimson*, October 29, 2009. http://www.thecrimson.com/article/2009/10/29/ghosts-thayer-up-nbsp.

Shay, Andrea. "A Playwright's Benevolent Ghost Still Haunts BU's Halls." *WBUR Boston's NPR Station*. October 30, 2009. http://www.wbur.org/2009/10/30/haunted-dorm.

Siena-Bivona, Ginnie, Dorothy McConachie and Mitchel Whitington. *Real-Life Stories of Supernatural Experiences*. Dallas, TX: Atriad, 2003.

"Spirit Reflections—Ghosts and Haunted Mirrors." *HubPages*. http://seeker7.hubpages.com/hub/Spirit-Reflections-Ghosts-and-Haunted-Mirrors.

Swayne, M.L. *America's Haunted Universities: Ghosts That Roam Hallowed Halls*. Woodbury, MN: Llewellyn Publications, 2012.

Tucker, Elizabeth. *Haunted Halls: Ghostlore of American College Campuses*. Jackson: University of Mississippi, 2007.

Varner, Marcus. "The Bride of College Ghost Stories: A Terrifying Trilogy." *Colleges and Careers*. October 24, 2007. http://www.classesandcareers.com/education/2007/10/24/the-bride-of-college-ghost-stories-a-terrifying-trilogy.

Wainwright, Charles E. "Old Friends: Robin Mingo and Nathan Dane." *Historically Speaking*, July 24, 2011. http://history.firstparishbeverly.org/archives/22.

"What to Do If Your House Is Haunted." *Anderson Cooper*. October 31, 2011. http://www.andersoncooper.com/2011/10/28/what-to-do-if-your-house-is-haunted.

Websites

TheBridgewaterTriangle.com
CastleofSpirits.com
CelebrateBoston.com
CollegeConfidential.com
CollegeProwler.com
ForgottenUSA.com
GhostCircle.com
Ghost-Mysteries.com
GhostsofAmerica.com
GhostVillage.com
HauntedMHC.blogspot.com
Hauntin.gs
HollowHill.com
TheShadowLands.net
StrangeUSA.com
Wikipedia.org

ABOUT THE AUTHOR

R enee Mallett is the author of *Manchester Ghosts* and several other books about ghosts and legends in the New England states. She has published numerous pieces of writing ranging from short fiction to poetry and celebrity interviews to travel essays.

Renee Mallett lives in southern New Hampshire with her family. Readers are invited to visit her studio at Western Avenue Studios, located at 122 Western Avenue in Lowell, Massachusetts, the first Saturday of each month for Open Studios. Or you can visit her on the web anytime at www.ReneeMallett.com